Christmas In Dairyland

For:
Millton Public Library

Happy Reading!

Jean R Ralph

Colfax, Wisconsin

Oct. 14, 2003

Christmas In Dairyland

True Stories From a Wisconsin Farm

LeAnn R. Ralph

In memory of my mother, Norma Irene Halvorson Ralph (1916-1985) and in memory my father, Roy Arthur Ralph (1914-1992).

And for the dairy farmers of Wisconsin—and all farmers everywhere.

~ About the Cover ~

When I was a kid, Christmas would not have been Christmas without cookies. The cookie cutters pictured on the front cover are the ones we used at home on the farm. They are well over forty years old now, and I am still using them. Notice the dents in the handle of the star and the bell.

****

~ Foreword ~

Forty years ago when I was a little girl growing up on our dairy farm in west central Wisconsin, I thought everyone lived on a farm. Then again, many of my kindergarten classmates lived on farms, too, so maybe I wasn't completely off base.

Later on, however, after I had graduated from high school and started traveling around the United States, I was hard-pressed to meet anyone who had ever been on a dairy farm, much less lived on one. People would ask me where I was from and when I told them Wisconsin, they'd say, "I suppose you lived on a dairy farm."

After a while, it became clear to me that for people in other states, 'Wisconsin' and 'dairy farm' were synonymous. I would explain that not everyone in Wisconsin lives on a dairy farm, and then I would find myself answering questions about what it was like growing up on a farm.

Today, most of the small family dairy farms like the one where I grew up are gone. My parents milked 20 cows, but farmers can no longer make a living that way. Milk prices have essentially stayed the same since the 1970s, and many small farmers decided to sell their dairy herds when their business expenses ended up exceeding their gross farm income year after year.

Even though most of the small family farms have disappeared, the evidence that they once existed remains—in the empty dairy barns scattered around the countryside—in the pastures that have been turned into residential subdivisions—in the creameries that have been abandoned or converted into other uses.

And in my stories about growing up on a Wisconsin dairy farm.

LeAnn R. Ralph
Colfax, Wisconsin

~ 1 ~
The Lefse Connection

The school bus doors clattered shut behind me. "I wish it didn't get dark so soon," I muttered as the bus started backing out of the driveway.

Sunset arrived early on December afternoons, and even though it was only quarter after four, the sun was already hovering close to the horizon. Too close.

If I wanted to make a few sled runs down the driveway before dark, I would have to hurry. The plaid skirt, white blouse and red knee socks I was wearing wouldn't be any good for sledding, and before I could play outside in the snow, I would have to change my clothes.

The empty feeling in the pit of my stomach reminded me that I would also have to eat a quick snack. Maybe there were still some of those oatmeal cookies left that my big sister, Loretta, had baked last weekend.

I took a firmer grip on my books, and as the bus headed back out to the main road a half a mile away, I started toward the house. So far today, the milk truck was the only vehicle which had driven up and down our hill through the couple of inches of snow that had fallen last night.

If we got more than a few inches, Dad would use the tractor and bucket to clear the driveway. But after a big storm, when there were sometimes drifts almost as high as the third wire on the pasture fence, the milk truck driver would use a blade mounted on the front of the truck to plow his way up the hill. The two or three inches on the driveway now, though, wasn't nearly enough for either Dad or the milk hauler to bother plowing.

Not that it made any difference whether the driveway was plowed. It had already snowed a few inches several times this winter, and underneath the layer of fresh snow was a surface packed smooth by the weight of cars and trucks driving up and down the hill. When I hopped on my sled and pushed off, it would travel from the top of the driveway all the way to road below, moving at a rate of speed that was fast as our dog,

Needles, when one of the cows chased him. And if a cow thought Needles was too close to her calf, he could run awfully fast.

Needles was a Cocker Spaniel-Spitz mix, who, when he was a puppy, had nipped my sister's ankles while she was hanging clothes outside to dry. Loretta had exclaimed, "Get those needles out of here!" And the name had stuck.

As I rounded the curve by the willow tree growing in the lawn, I saw my sled leaning against the porch railing. Dad had braided three pieces of twine string together so I could steer my sled when I went down the hill and so I could pull the sled behind me when I climbed back up the hill.

Twine string, I had discovered, was an extremely useful item. When it wasn't holding bales of hay together, you could use it for all sorts of things. To make reins when you wanted to ride your favorite cow. As a toy you could twitch across the barn floor so the kitties would chase it. As a leash for your dog when you went to the feed mill with your dad. And as a rope for your sled.

When I reached the top of the hill, I turned toward the house. During the last few minutes, the sun had slipped closer to the horizon, and the slanting red rays threw a pink tint across the white snow and the house and the barn and the garage. It would be dark soon, but in just about five minutes, or maybe even less, I would be racing down the hill on my sled.

I climbed the porch steps, opened the door—and forgot all about playing in the snow.

I sniffed once...twice...then I hastily set down my books and removed my boots, shivering when my red socks touched the cold concrete porch floor.

Moments later when I opened the kitchen door, the mouth-watering aroma of potatoes and butter grew stronger. The kitchen counter was covered with flour, and there stood Mom, her face flushed from the heat of the lefse griddle. A spatula in one hand, her other hand gripped the edge of the stove. A snow-white dishtowel lay folded around the lefse she had already baked.

Every year, Mom made lefse for Christmas. In my opinion, the flat potato pastry (pronounced lef'-suh) that had been brought to this country by Norwegian immigrants, was better, even, than Christmas cookies. By itself, lefse didn't really taste like much, but once it was spread with butter, sprinkled with sugar and rolled into a log, I would have happily eaten nothing but lefse for breakfast, dinner and supper.

Lefse also played a big part in the lunches served following our Sunday school Christmas program. The church was only a half mile from our farm, and Mom had told me once that her parents, grandparents, aunts, and uncles had been among those who had founded the little white country church.

After spending an hour during the Christmas program listening to us mumble our Bible verses and sing songs off key, such as *Away in a Manger* and *O Little Town of Bethlehem* and *We Three Kings of Orient Are*, the congregation went downstairs for lunch. Next to the Christmas cookies and the open-faced Cheese-Whiz-and-crushed-potato-chip-on-nutbread-sandwiches were plates of lefse and other Norwegian delicacies. Lunch would not have been lunch without lefse, sandbakelse (sunbuckles), krumkake (kroom-kaka or kroom-kaga) and fattigman (futtymun).

Seeing as I felt the way I did about lefse, it was lucky for me that my mother was the daughter of Norwegian immigrants.

The farm where we lived had been homesteaded by my great-grandfather in the late 1800s. Although they spoke only Norwegian at home when Mom was growing up, she was familiar with the way English sounded because her father could speak it very well. Grandpa Nils came to this country when he was a little boy, so he possessed a good grasp of 'American,' Mom said, which was a funny way, I thought, of referring to English.

My mother had explained that her parents had called the language 'American' to distinguish it from 'British English'—two distinct languages as far as they were concerned.

My maternal grandmother, Inga, arrived here when she was an adult. She did not speak American very well. Or so she claimed. Mom said she suspected her mother understood English a whole lot better than she let on.

And like all good Norwegians, my mother had learned to make lefse.

But then, when she was twenty-six years old, Mom contracted polio. The disease left her completely paralyzed in her left leg and partially paralyzed in her right. She walked with crutches most of the time, but around the house, she used furniture and the kitchen counters to support herself.

My mother was forty-two when I was born. After the polio, the doctors told her she would never have any more children. And she didn't—not until sixteen years later. My sister, Loretta, is nineteen years older than I am and my brother, Ingman, who was named for our grandmother, Inga, is twenty-one years older.

Two years after my sister, another boy who had been named Charles was born with a cleft palate. The local doctor planned to take him to a hospital in the Twin Cities for surgery. Before the baby left on his hundred-mile journey, Mom wanted him baptized.

The day the minister was coming to the house, my mother woke up in the morning and could not hear Charles' raspy breathing. She knew—before she even got out of bed—that the baby had died during the night. Not long after that, she had been stricken with polio.

Because of the paralysis, my mother couldn't drive, which meant if she wanted to go somewhere, she had to wait until my father or sister or brother could take her. She couldn't run up and down the stairs, either, but instead, had to crawl on her hands and knees. And she most certainly could not walk down the hill of our driveway to get the mail.

To wash dishes, my mother leaned on her elbows or forearms and moved only her hands. For cooking, she hung onto the counter with her left hand and used her right hand to prepare the food. If there was a task that she could do sitting down (peeling potatoes, putting bread dough into pans, or frosting a cake), she would sit by the table to do her work.

And yet, in spite of her physical limitations, my mother recognized that her family liked lefse, and so she made it.

Lefse is a mixture of mashed or riced potatoes, flour, milk and melted butter rolled into large, thin pieces. The fragile pastry is placed on a 500-degree griddle where it is baked for a minute or so until it develops brown freckles; then it's flipped over and baked on the other side.

Many times when I came home from school on a December afternoon, I would discover that my mother was making lefse.

And so it was today.

As I closed the porch door behind me, Mom placed another piece of lefse under the dishtowel and then glanced at the kitchen clock.

"Home already?" she asked.

I craned my neck to see the clock, too. The old butter-yellow Time-A-Trol that had been installed by the electric company before I was born read 4:20.

"Same as usual," I said, setting my books on the table.

"I guess I've been so busy I didn't realize it was getting late," Mom said. "Want some lefse?"

By way of a reply, I lifted a corner of the dishtowel and reached for the butter dish.

My mother always kept a plentiful supply of butter. She ordered it from the milk hauler—who brought it with him on his rounds from the creamery in town six miles away—because butter was about half the price of store-bought that way and as economical as margarine. No one in our family could have been persuaded to eat margarine, though. I had only heard Mom and Dad mention the word 'oleo' a couple of times. 'Oleo' was uttered in such a way that I knew better than to ask any questions.

I took a piece of warm lefse off the pile and placed it on the cupboard. Then I slathered it with butter and sprinkled it liberally with sugar and cinnamon. Among lefse-eaters there is some disagreement about whether cinnamon is acceptable. My mother always ate her lefse with cinnamon. I had grown up eating my lefse with cinnamon. I liked it with cinnamon.

I rolled the flat piece of lefse into a log and carefully lifted it to my mouth so the sugar and cinnamon wouldn't spill out the end.

I bit.

I chewed.

I swallowed.

And then I took another big bite.

Oh, this was good. Tender and sweet. It tasted as heavenly as any lefse I had ever eaten.

"Is it all right?" Mom asked, watching me out of the corner of her eye.

"Hmmm-hmm."

"Good," she replied, moving another piece of raw lefse dough toward the griddle.

Suddenly my mother yanked her hand back and the pancake turner that had been sitting on the cupboard clattered to the floor. Mom used a pancake turner because she said the long, flat, wooden turners that were supposed to be used for turning lefse were too awkward for her to handle.

"Ouch!" she cried.

"Whas-sa-matter?" I mumbled around another mouthful of lefse.

My mother struggled to move the dough off the cupboard and onto the griddle. Then she turned her arm to look at an ugly red welt that was already beginning to blister.

"Burned myself," she replied. "Again."

She held up her arm so I could see the three big, red welts she had acquired that afternoon.

Every time Mom made lefse, she burned herself. Sometimes she burned the underside of her arm. Sometimes the top side. Sometimes her fingers. As she tried to keep her balance by holding onto the kitchen counter while at the same time moving the raw lefse dough to the griddle, she couldn't seem to avoid getting burned.

"Oh, Mom," I said, knowing that the blistered burns would take weeks to heal and fade away.

"Well...," she admitted, "it does hurt a little. I'll put some of that pink salve on it after a while. It'll be all right."

The pink salve, which came in a small round tin container and smelled like wintergreen, was good for skinned elbows and knees, too. And I knew plenty about skinned elbows and knees. Even though playing jump rope with my friends at school was tremendous fun, it was also sometimes dangerous.

I finished my piece of lefse and reached for another.

Mom glanced at me and smiled.

"You must be hungry today," she commented.

But when I reached for the third piece, my mother frowned.

"Don't eat too much of that," she cautioned.

"Why not?" I asked, applying butter in a thick layer.

"Because you won't be hungry for supper—that's why."

So my third piece of lefse ended up being the last one. For now.

My mother always claimed she wasn't any good at making lefse. That it was much thicker and smaller than it should have been. That the lefse the ladies served at church after our Christmas program every year, which was three times the size of my mother's pancake-like pieces and nearly thin enough to see through, was the way lefse was supposed to look.

The way it was 'supposed' to look? Who cared about the way it was supposed to look? As far as I was concerned, Mom's lefse was the best I had ever eaten.

I went upstairs to change out of my school clothes. From my bedroom window I saw that the sun had already set and it was starting to get dark.

No sledding for me today. But I didn't mind. Mom was baking lefse! And that meant Christmas was almost here.

****

Directions for making lefse are included in Appendix A, where you will also find recipes for other traditional Norwegian Christmas goodies including julekake, Christmas bread, fattigman, and sot suppe (sweet soup).

~ 2 ~
Dad's Favorite Christmas Present

My mother held up a package wrapped in white butcher paper that she had just taken out of a brown paper grocery bag. "What is this?" she asked.

I had arrived home from school only a couple of minutes ago. My father had gone to town to grind feed this afternoon, and as she often did, Mom asked him to pick up a few things at the store while he was in town.

Three or four trucks must have been ahead of Dad at the feed mill because he came home as I was walking up the hill after getting off the school bus. My father preferred to be home earlier than this so he could start chores at the normal time. Either he was going to have hurry while he was feeding the cows, or else supper was going to be late.

Dad glanced at the wrapped package my mother held.

"What is it? That's my Christmas present," he replied, as he reached for his chore cap. As usual, Dad was dressed in blue overalls and a blue chambray work shirt. Even during the winter, his face never lost the tan that he acquired from driving the tractor all summer long.

"Your *Christmas* present?" I asked.

Christmas was still a few weeks away, but upstairs two presents for Dad were hidden in my dresser drawer. I knew that my sister, Loretta, had already wrapped a couple of packages for him, too.

"Nobody else will buy it for me," Dad continued, "so I figured I'd get it for myself."

Mom quickly dropped the parcel onto the cupboard, as if it had burned her fingers. "That's not what I think it is—is it?"

Dad grinned. "I don't know," he said. "What do you think it is?"

My curiosity got the better of me. First Dad bought himself a Christmas present and now Mom wore the same look on her face as she did after discovering she had forgotten about a container of leftovers that had been pushed to the back of the refrigerator a month ago.

The white package, I noticed, was just about the same size as the packages of hamburger which came from the meat locker in town. "What is it, Daddy?" I asked.

My father picked up the parcel in one work-roughened hand and reached for the refrigerator door with the other. "You'll find out later," he said.

My mother grasped the kitchen counter more tightly and drew herself up straight to her full five feet and seven inches. Her blue eyes became steely.

"Hold it right there, mister. You are NOT putting that in MY refrigerator."

"I'm not?" Dad asked. He turned toward her.

"No—absolutely not." Standing with her knees locked tightly, she grasped the edge of the cupboard door and leaned down to retrieve a clean empty coffee can from beneath the kitchen sink.

Mom didn't believe in throwing away perfectly good coffee cans. We used them to make berry picking pails in the summer. Dad also used them to sprinkle lime on the barn floor and as watering cans for the garden after he had punched holes in the bottom. Sometimes he pinched one side together to form a spout and then he used the can to pour oil or hydraulic fluid into the tractor.

Mom held the coffee can toward Dad. "Here. You can keep it in this."

My father looked at the container. "But why do I have to keep it in a coffee can?"

"Because," Mom said. "You do."

Dad sighed. He put the package inside the can and replaced the cover. Once again he reached for the refrigerator door.

"Tut-tut!" Mom exclaimed.

"*Now* what's the matter?"

"You are *not* keeping that up here," she declared.

"I'm not? Not even in a coffee can? With the cover on tight?"

"Nope," Mom replied.

"Then where am I *supposed* to keep it?"

"In the basement," she said.

I looked back and forth between the two of them. Mom and Loretta used all kinds of secret hiding places for Christmas presents, but no present had ever been put in the basement.

"How come Daddy has to keep his present in the basement?"

Neither one of them answered my question, although my father looked like a man who knew he had lost the battle.

"Okay, Ma. You win."

I followed Dad downstairs where he set the can on a shelf.

"But—what is it Daddy?"

"The best thing in the world," he replied. "And right after milking, I'm gonna make a sandwich."

"Is it sandwich meat then?"

"Better. It's cheese."

Cheese? Now why in the world would Mom make Dad keep cheese in the basement? We didn't keep other kinds of cheese in the basement, even though the basement always stayed cool. Mom said the little square space in the sandstone wall was a 'refrigerator' of sorts, and that when she was a girl, they used to keep their milk and butter there. The basement walls were constructed of sandstone blocks that my great-grandfather had quarried from the hill behind our barn.

That evening after milking, my father went downstairs to get his coffee can. Every evening after milking, he ate a snack. My father was five feet, ten inches tall, weighed one-hundred-and-fifty pounds, and was the strongest person I knew, next to my brother, Ingman. Dad was forty-four when I was born, and when he threw a sixty-pound bale of hay, it seemed to float through the air, almost as if he hadn't expended any effort at all, and landed neatly in the exact spot where he had intended it to land.

When Dad arrived back in the kitchen, he set the coffee can on the kitchen counter and then reached into the bottom cupboard for an onion. He rummaged around in the utensil drawer until he found a paring knife, and then he began to remove the onion's brittle orangish-yellow outer layer.

My mother was sitting at the table, paging through the newspaper. Her naturally curly hair was so dark brown that it looked more black than brown. Dad, Loretta and Ingman had dark hair too. I was only the blond-haired person in the family, although we all had blue eyes. One time I had asked Mom why I had blond hair, and she said it was the same color as her mother's hair had been.

My mother stopped perusing the newspaper. "You're going to have raw onion on it, too?" she asked, dark eyebrows arched high on her forehead.

Dad began slicing the onion. "Of course. Gotta have onion on my sandwich."

"Well at least let me get out of the kitchen first before you start eating that," Mom declared, reaching for her crutches.

Meanwhile, Dad opened the coffee can, pulled out the parcel and peeled back the white paper. My mother cast a single, worried look over her shoulder just before she disappeared into the living room. I leaned closer. I took yet another step closer as he began to cut a slice.

Suddenly, a horrible odor struck my nose. I hastily stepped back and pinched my nostrils shut.

Before I had time to say anything, I heard my sister's voice from upstairs. "What," she said, "is that *awful* smell."

The bedroom I shared with my sister was right above the kitchen at the top of the stairs. On any other day of the week, Loretta would have been staying at the apartment she rented in the city where she worked. Today was Friday, so she was home for the weekend.

"Dad," I gasped, "what kind of cheese IS that?"

It sort of smelled like a mouse had crawled into the coffee can and died. A week ago. At least. Or maybe two. And I knew full well what dead mouse smelled like. One time a mouse had died in the little storage space under the stairway that Mom called the 'pantry.' As soon we could smell the odor, my mother had pulled everything out of the pantry, including the big pot she used for making jelly and the tall canister used for storing Christmas cookies, so she could dispose of the tiny carcass. Then she had scrubbed the pantry's wooden floor and walls with pine cleaner.

A dead mouse in the pantry had not smelled quite as unappetizing as this. Or maybe it only seemed that way because the dead-mouse-in-the-pantry episode had happened a long time ago, but the smell of the cheese was in the kitchen right now.

"It's called Limburger," Dad explained happily, putting the onion on top of the cheese. He buttered another slice of bread to complete his sandwich, and then he bit into it. A blissful expression appeared on his face as he chewed and swallowed.

He paused before taking the next bite and held the sandwich toward me. "Want to taste it?"

I backed away, shaking my head. "Errrr—uh—no thanks, Daddy."

I quickly joined Mom in the living room. But even from there, we could still smell the Limburger.

When Dad had finished his sandwich, Mom told me to go to the kitchen and pour some of the pine cleaner into the sink, hoping that it would cover up the odor.

The pine cleaner helped, but it was another ten minutes before we were reasonably sure we couldn't smell the cheese anymore.

Every evening after that until the Limburger was gone, Dad made a sandwich. I never asked him why he liked Limburger so much. I figured it was just one of those strange things adults did that I would not understand anyway, although I remember him saying his Grandma Zinderman, a person he described as a small tough-as-nails German woman, liked Limburger too. Dad and some of his sisters had lived with their grandmother for a while when they were growing up.

As for me, at least the mystery was solved of why my mother insisted that Dad had to keep his 'Christmas present' in the basement.

And I no longer wondered, either, why he had to buy it for himself.

****

~ 3 ~
Rushing The Season

Every year when November arrived, I started to wonder when it would snow.

And this year was no exception.

Thanksgiving was only a week and a half away, and we still didn't have any snow on the ground yet.

Mom and Dad had arrived home from grocery shopping a few minutes ago. Since my mother couldn't drive because of the polio, Dad would take her into town and help her with the shopping. Although today happened to be Saturday, a trip to town for groceries could occur on any day of the week (except Sunday), all depending upon the farm work.

During the summer, Mom and Dad went to town on rainy days when Dad couldn't be out in the field cutting, raking or baling hay. During the winter, their trips to town were on days when it wasn't snowing and when it wasn't below zero. My mother didn't like to go outside when it was below zero. She said the polio paralysis caused her to have poor circulation and that she was afraid she would get frostbite.

On my way across the yard, I zipped up the lined denim jacket that I wore for helping Dad with the chores. I had remembered to grab my stocking cap before leaving the house, but I had neglected to take my mittens. A cold east wind quickly turned my hands into what felt like little blocks of ice.

Yesterday morning the sky had been bright and sunny, but by afternoon, a thin layer of hazy clouds made the sun look like someone had covered it with gauze. Today, the sky was filled with low gray clouds that seemed as if they were only a few feet above the treetops on the hill behind our barn.

"Think you can carry this?" Dad asked when I reached the car. He held out a brown paper bag.

"What's in it?"

"Oh," he said, lifting the bag up, as if to test the weight, "about twenty pounds, I guess."

"Twenty pounds?"

"That's our turkey," Mom explained. "For Thanksgiving. Take it out to the freezer, please."

The air felt so cold that I was pretty sure we could leave the turkey outside on the porch and it would stay frozen. But I also knew that if we left the turkey outside, our dog, Needles—or the barn cats—would have a grand time feasting on frozen turkey. Or least they would try to have a grand time feasting on frozen turkey. No one had to tell me that tooth marks in our turkey wouldn't make my mother very happy.

I grabbed the grocery bag that Dad held, hoping the handles wouldn't break. No one had to tell me that dropping the turkey in the dirt wouldn't sit too well with Mom, either.

Before I reached the machine shed where we kept the chest freezer, something cold and wet landed on my cheek and then on my nose and lips.

I could hardly believe my eyes.

It was a snowing!

By the time I had rearranged some packages of green beans and sweetcorn to make room in the freezer for the turkey and had carefully shut, and latched the door of the little room Dad had built around the freezer to keep out the dust and dirt, the ground was already covered with a thin layer of white.

On my way back to the car, I glanced across the yard and noticed it was so snowing so hard I could barely see the woods across the road at the back of our neighbor's farm .

Last year we had gotten a snowstorm before Thanksgiving too.

And then I remembered something else.

Every year, Dad and I went to one of our pine plantations to cut a Christmas tree. The trees had been planted on dry, sandy slopes to stop soil erosion. A few times when we went on our annual Christmas tree expedition, there was no snow at all, but more often than not, we had at least a few inches. Last year, it had started snowing before Thanksgiving, and by the middle of December, we had more snow on the ground than we sometimes got all year, making it almost impossible to drive through our fields to reach the pine plantation.

'What if we get that much snow again this year?' I wondered as I lifted the trunk lid and took out the last two bags of groceries.

I shut the trunk, and then I turned and headed toward the house.

Mom was putting away groceries and Dad was changing into his work shoes when I walked into the kitchen.

"Dad, when can we get a Christmas tree?" I asked, as I closed the door behind me. My hands still felt like little blocks of ice, although I figured they would be warm again soon now that I was back in the house.

Before my father could reply, Mom spoke up. She was holding a can of cranberry sauce that she had intended to put in the cupboard. Instead, she set it down on the counter with a firm thump.

"Christmas tree?" she said. "It's not even Thanksgiving!"

"But —"

"I WON'T have a Christmas tree before the middle of December," she continued, warming to the subject.

"But—"

"Christmas tree! The very idea. Turkey's not even thawed and she's talking about a Christmas tree."

As I set the two bags of groceries on the table, Dad and I exchanged glances. For as long as I could remember, I had known that my mother did not believe it was proper to put up a Christmas tree until well into December. I hadn't realized she would react this way, though.

"But Mom—"

"Don't you 'but Mom' me. If I had my way, we wouldn't decorate our tree until Christmas Eve. It's ridiculous the way they keep trying to stretch out the Christmas season. The next thing you know, we'll be starting our Christmas shopping before Halloween. A tree! In November!"

"Ma," Dad said quietly. "Don't you want to hear what she has to say?"

"Christmas tree! I haven't hardly had time to think about Thanksgiving, much less Christmas! Which reminds me. We forgot to buy sweet potatoes. If we're going to have sweet potatoes for Thanksgiving, someone is going to have to make another trip to the store. Unless we want to skip them for Thanksgiving and have them at Christmas instead. Although, come to think of it, I don't know why I should even bother with Thanksgiving. A Christmas tree! In November!"

Dad looked at me and sighed.

"Getting a Christmas tree *now* is almost as bad as those guys who bought trees from us one year so they could sell them at Christmas!" Mom exclaimed as she made her way over to the table to sit down. "Said they had to cut them early. I'll say it was early. September, no less. I've always pitied the poor people who bought those trees. Must have been all dried out and absolutely good for nothing by Christmas."

Dad cleared his throat.

As Mom drew another deep breath, she glanced at me. "Oh, all right. I suppose I should let you get a word in edgewise. What about a Christmas tree?"

"I just thought," I said meekly, "that if we get our tree right after Thanksgiving this year, we probably won't have so much snow."

"That's right," Dad added. "Last year, we waited until the middle of December and we couldn't take the pickup. Even had trouble getting the tractor back in the field. We almost got stuck."

"Hmmphhh! A Christmas tree!" Mom grumbled. "The very idea. In November!"

"But Mom," I said, "look at how hard it's snowing."

"A Christmas tree," she muttered. "The next thing you know, she'll be pestering me about decorating it the day after Thanksgiving!"

After a while, my mother finally calmed down. Dad and I didn't dare mention cutting a tree again until December, and by that time there was so much snow, it wasn't a matter of 'almost' getting stuck with the tractor, we did get stuck, even with chains on the tires.

Dad was pretty upset about it, too. It was one thing to get stuck with the pickup because you could always pull the truck out with the tractor. But what do you do when the tractor is stuck?

You shovel an awful lot of snow away from the tires, that's what...

****

~ 4 ~
They're Here!

In a few minutes the bell would ring, and just like everyone else in my grade school class, I was busy taking off my coat and mittens and boots and hurrying to put them away.

There was only one problem.

Hanging up our coats in the little closet hidden by a sliding bulletin board was not as easy as it sounded.

Actually, hanging up the coats was easy enough—it was closing the closet door that proved difficult.

Each week, two people were assigned to open and close the coat closet. This week it was me and a boy in our class who was famous for getting the giggles.

When my classmates and I had worn sweaters earlier in the fall, the door slid down with the ease of Dad's freshly-sharpened pocket knife slicing through the twine string on a bale of hay. Now that we all wore heavy winter coats, no sooner would we start to pull the door shut when one of the coats would fall off its hook. We would hang the coat up again, but as soon as we started to pull the door down, another coat would fall off.

At first our predicament was funny, although as the minutes ticked by neither one of us felt like laughing anymore. The rule was that the coat closet had to be shut by the time the bell rang to announce the start of the school day. And the bell had already rung about two minutes ago.

"Well, that certainly wasn't a very good way to start off on a Monday morning, was it," our teacher said when we had finally succeeded in closing the closet door and were settled into our seats. Then she smiled so we knew we weren't in trouble.

It wasn't just any old Monday morning, however. It was the Monday following Thanksgiving vacation. Coming back to school after the free-dom of a weekend was always tough, but following the four-day break for Thanksgiving, well…let's just say I would rather not be here at all. Not when I could be at home on the farm where there was always something fun to do: feeding the calves, or going to town with Dad to grind feed, or riding my sled down our driveway.

Earlier that morning while I ate breakfast, Mom had tried to make me feel better about school by reminding me that Christmas vacation was only a few weeks away. To me, the time seemed more like months—or maybe even years—rather than a few weeks.

As it turned out, closing the closet door was the highlight of the morning. After that it was the same old thing. Working on arithmetic problems, completing spelling book exercises to help us learn this week's list of words, and filling out vocabulary worksheets.

When lunch was over, the second half of the day held even less promise than the first half. Especially after our teacher informed us that once we finished working in our reading groups, we would start the next chapter in the social studies book.

Most of the time the social studies book represented nothing more than a bunch of facts that had nothing to do with me. Senators? Representatives? Governors? The President of the United States? All of those people lived a long, long, long ways off, and it wasn't as if I were ever going to see any of them in person.

The time spent in our reading groups, on the other hand, always went quickly. Maybe that's because we took turns reading out loud and helped each other answer questions about the story. Any activity where we could work together was more fun than working alone.

We had finished answering the last question about the story and were considering asking our teacher if we could do the next story when she announced that it was time for social studies. Reluctantly, I picked up my chair and returned to my desk.

I was still trying to find my social studies book when our teacher asked for a volunteer to run an errand for her at the office. Two dozen arms shot into the air, waving wildly. The teacher selected a girl who sat right across from me, and as my classmate triumphantly left the room, I returned to finding my book, finding the right page, and wondering how long it would take to read the chapter.

I had managed to make it through the first page and had started on the second one when my classmate returned from her errand.

"They're here!" she whispered, as she plopped down at her desk just across the aisle from mine.

I turned to look at her. So did some of the other kids who sat near us.

"What's here?" someone finally whispered back.

"The Christmas trees," she hissed. "I saw the truck parked outside. They're starting to unload them!"

The Christmas trees!

Every year soon after Thanksgiving, a truck delivered Christmas trees to our school, one tree for each room, and soon the whispered refrain of "They're here! The Christmas trees are here!" was making its way up and down the aisles.

Our classroom was on the side of the building facing the driveway, and if you sat close to the windows, you could accidentally wander by them on your way to or from the pencil sharpener. And suddenly it seemed there was an epidemic of dull pencils that urgently needed sharpening. Not everyone was lucky enough to sit close to the windows, and those who didn't waited impatiently for the latest news.

"The principal's standing on the sidewalk watching them take the trees off the truck," came one whispered report.

"The janitor's helping them, too," came another report.

"The principal went back inside," came a third report.

"They're finished. The truck just left," came a fourth report.

"I saw the janitor carrying a Christmas tree inside!" said a fifth.

We knew, then, that it was only a matter of time until we heard a knock on the door.

When that much-anticipated knock finally arrived, an uncharacteristic silence descended upon the class. Not a word was whispered, not a paper rustled, not a pencil tapped during those few seconds between the time our teacher opened the door until the janitor started backing into the room.

"Where should I put your Christmas tree?" he asked cheerfully after he and the bushy evergreen had made it through the door mostly in one piece. The janitor's cap had fallen off, and a few pine needles were scattered on the floor around his feet. I knew that later on, there would be a race to see who could reach the pine needles first. Those who were successful would crush them between their fingers to smell the pine scent.

Our teacher opened her closet and brought out a tree stand while the janitor selected several of the bigger boys to hold the tree upright while he crawled underneath to turn the screws.

The janitor who delivered our tree was none other than Mike Flynn. Each year on St. Patrick's Day, Mr. Flynn brought his shillelagh to school and visited all of the rooms to tell us he wasn't Mike Flynn that day but had been turned into a leprechaun overnight.

Since most of us were of Norwegian or German descent, the first time Mike Flynn said he had been turned into a leprechaun, we didn't know what he was talking about until he explained that he and his shillelagh could do magic. At least for St. Patty's Day. None of us had ever seen a shillelagh. The polished walking stick Mike carried obviously had been a small tree branch at one time, but now it was so smooth to the touch that you could just about feel the magic radiating from it.

Mike Flynn almost certainly played a prominent role at Christmas, too. On the last day before Christmas vacation, Santa Claus would mysteriously appear in our midst to deliver small paper bags of candy and peanuts to each classroom. Although we were pretty sure it was Mike Flynn in a Santa suit, complete with a long, white, curly beard and a couple of pillows to fill out the jacket, he made the most convincing Santa Claus we had ever seen.

In a few minutes, Mr. Flynn and the boys had put the tree into the stand.

"Let's set it back in this corner for the time being," said the teacher, leading the way.

"And would you be sure, now, that this is where you want it?" Mike asked as he peered through the branches at our teacher.

"Yes, this is fine," she said.

Mr. Flynn set the tree down and then he turned to leave. "I've got six more to deliver, so I'd best be on my way. Merrrrrry Christmas!! Ho-ho-ho!"

"Thank you, Mr. Flynn," said our teacher, giving us a meaningful glance.

"Thank you, Mr. Flynn," we chorused.

"You're ever so welcome!" he said, striding jauntily to the door.

Mike Flynn was not an especially tall man, but what he lacked in height he more than made up for in personality.

By the time the janitor left, our teacher knew it was useless to continue with social studies. So instead, she started directing the rearrangement of our desks. Other years we had pulled our desks forward to make more room for the tree in the back, or else we had pushed our desks backward to make more room in the front. This year, we put our desks into a circle. Then the teacher called on a couple of boys who pushed, pulled and dragged our Christmas tree until it was in the center of the room.

When we were finished rearranging our desks and moving the tree, it was almost time for the final bell.

"We'll decorate our tree tomorrow," the teacher announced.

Tomorrow?

At first I thought I must have misunderstood. Last year, our teacher had insisted that we wait until Friday afternoon, even though the tree had been delivered on Wednesday. As excited whispers of, "she said we could decorate the tree tomorrow!" swirled around me, I knew my ears hadn't been playing tricks.

The next morning, I was ready and waiting for the bus about ten minutes earlier than usual. Normally I did not feel much of a sense of urgency about going to school, and my mother often had to prod me into finishing my breakfast, brushing my teeth and getting dressed.

"Are you sure you feel all right?" Mom asked, as I stood in the living room next to the picture window. Because of the way the road and the hills were situated, we could see the bus when it was still on the main highway a little more than a half a mile away, leaving me just enough time to walk down the driveway to meet it.

"I feel fine, Mom. Why?" I asked, turning toward her.

She shook her head and shrugged. "Because you're ready so early, that's why. And since it's out of character for you—you must be sick."

"We're going to decorate the Christmas tree today, remember?"

A bemused smile touched the corners of my mother's lips. "You are? I guess I *do* seem to recall that you mentioned something about it last night. I didn't catch all of it."

In reality, I had dominated the suppertime conversation by giving a full account of the tree's delivery to our room and the way in which we had moved our desks into a circle. I had also informed Mom and Dad that our teacher said we could decorate the tree on Tuesday when our teacher last year had made us wait until Friday. Most of our teachers believed that we could not concentrate very well on Friday afternoons, so they reserved the last half a day of the week for activities such as spelling bees, math games, word games—or decorating the Christmas tree.

After I caught a glimpse of the bus on the main highway, I hurried out of the house and down the hill. Then I waited impatiently until the bus pulled up. Even before the door had opened completely, I was already climbing the steps.

Our farm was one of the first stops on the route, which meant I had a long ride to school. Although nothing out of the ordinary occurred (no flat tires; no cows out in the middle of the road; no slippery spots that caused an unexpected side trip into the ditch), it seemed as if we were never going to reach our destination.

At last, the bus stopped in front of the school. I jumped to my feet and jostled my way down the long aisle with all of the other kids who were also trying to exit the bus as quickly as possible.

Eventually I made it to the sidewalk. Just before I reached the door of the school building, I heard someone shouting my name. It was one of my classmates.

"Look what I've got," she said breathlessly, running to catch up. She was carrying a large, brown paper bag. Nestled in crumpled sheets of newspaper were red, green, gold, blue and silver glass ball ornaments. The bag was nearly full.

"Where did those come from?" I asked.

"My mother said we could have them for school," my friend explained. Then she grinned. "That's because Mom wants to buy new ones for at home."

When we walked into our classroom a few minutes later, we discovered that several other kids had brought ornaments from home, too. Not nearly as many as my friend had brought, but enough all together so that we would have a 'real' Christmas tree rather than one which was decorated only with paper ornaments that we had made.

"Can we put these on the tree right now?" someone asked.

"Can we?"

"Pretty pleeeeease?"

"With sugar on top?"

Our teacher stopped writing on the blackboard and turned toward us. When she smiled, we exchanged eager, hopeful glances.

But then she shook her head.

"In the first place, MAY we—"

"MAY we put them on now?"

"Please?"

"Pretty pleeeeease?"

"Let's wait," she suggested. "We've still got to make the rest of our decorations."

"When are we going to do that?" someone asked.

"And what kind of decorations are we going to make?"

"Can we start now? I mean, *may* we start now? Pleeeease?"

She shook her head again. "No, no. We've got to at least get a little work done this morning. The tree can wait until this afternoon."

Somehow we made it through math and reading and music and lunch time.

When we were all settled into our desks again following the noon recess, some of my classmates set to work making chains out of slips of royal blue construction paper. In other years, the paper chains were always red and green. This year, our teacher said we could have red and green or else we could choose from royal blue, a pretty lilac purple, or bright pink. We took a vote, and royal blue had won by a solid majority.

While the paper chain crew worked at the counter, other students cut snowflakes from white paper. Still others strung popcorn our teacher had popped at home and had brought to school for us. One girl's mother had sent two bags of whole cranberries, so some of us (me, for one) strung cranberries instead of popcorn.

When everything was ready, we started decorating the tree. First came the snowflakes. Those who had made snowflakes carefully hung them on the tree by white strings that they had tied to the top.

Then came the ornaments. While the students who had brought them placed them on the tree, the rest of us kept a sharp eye on their progress so we didn't end up with too many in one place. The girl who had brought the paper bag full of ornaments asked the teacher if she could let everyone help. There were enough so that we each could put one on the tree. When we had finished, four were left, and we all agreed that the girl who had brought them should finish putting them on.

After that came the strings of popcorn and cranberries. My mother had told me that when she was a girl, they used to string popcorn for their tree at the one-room country school a mile from our farm. I had never heard of anyone stringing cranberries, and after we arranged them on the tree, I decided I very much liked the way they looked—red against the green, a little like a cardinal sitting in a pine tree. I had only seen one cardinal perched on a pine bough, and that had been at the back of our farm.

Last came the royal blue paper chains. By now the glue had dried, and the chains stayed together very well. One of my classmates had suggested setting them by the heat vent so they would dry faster, and it had been a brilliant idea. Last year the glue hadn't been dry, and the chains kept falling apart as they were placed on the tree.

One girl's mother had also sent tinsel, although at first our teacher said we couldn't use it. "It'll make such a mess, especially when the janitor takes the tree out of the room," she said. The beseeching looks of two dozen kids promising with all their hearts to remove *every bit* before the tree was taken down eventually overwhelmed her reluctance.

After the last strand of tinsel had been carefully placed, we returned to our desks. As we gazed at the tree, you could have heard a pine needle drop.

"Isn't it pretty?" someone finally said in a quiet voice.

"Lots prettier than last year when our chains kept falling apart," someone else said.

"I bet it will be the prettiest one in the whole *school*," declared a third.

No one said anything for a minute or two.

"How come you let us decorate the tree today?" someone asked eventually.

"Yeah, last year we had to wait until Friday."

"And today is only Tuesday."

The teacher shrugged "What else are we going to do with a perfectly good Christmas tree? If we waited until Friday, we would have just that many fewer days to enjoy it."

As I turned my attention once again to the snowflakes and ornaments and blue paper chains and popcorn and cranberries and tinsel that decorated our tree, it was as if someone had pulled open curtains to let bright sunshine into a darkened room.

The time between Thanksgiving and Christmas really was only a few short weeks, even though yesterday morning it had felt more like months.

But then, yesterday morning we didn't have a Christmas tree in our classroom.

Today we did.

And when there's a decorated tree in the middle of the room, everybody knows that Christmas vacation cannot be far behind.

****

~ 5 ~
Milkweed Pods and Poinsettias

Outside our classroom window, bright sunshine sparkled across the snow, and as I waited impatiently for the final bell to ring, I wondered if maybe Dad and I would cut a Christmas tree tomorrow. It was December, after all, and we had already decorated our classroom tree.

"I know it's Friday afternoon and that we've only got a few minutes of school left," said our teacher, "but I want you all to pay very close attention."

I turned away from the window and sat up straight.

When the teacher was sure that we were listening, she continued.

"This weekend, I want each of you to go out and find twenty-four milkweed pods. No, wait. Maybe you'd better make that thirty. A couple of them might get broken. And if you find a good supply and you'd like to bring extra in case someone else cannot find any, then please be sure you bring an additional thirty."

I exchanged glances with a couple my classmates.

"Thirty?" someone asked.

"Milkweed pods?" added another.

The teacher nodded. "Thirty milkweed pods."

"It's December. Aren't they all gone by now?" asked another classmate.

"The seeds are gone, but the pods will still be on the plants," the teacher said.

Over the years, our teachers had occasionally asked us to bring something to school—cream, for instance, when we were going to make butter, although only the kids who lived on farms were asked to bring cream. And one time we had to bring sugar cubes when we were going to make igloos. But so far, we'd never had to bring milkweed pods.

"Besides the milkweed pods, you will also need to bring a wire hanger to school on Monday," the teacher continued.

"Why do we need milkweed pods and hangers?" someone asked.

"Because we're going to make Christmas presents for your mothers," our teacher replied.

Every year, we made Christmas presents for our mothers. I always wondered why we made presents for our mothers and not for our fathers, too, although one year our teacher had helped us glue Popsicle sticks together to make frames for our school pictures, and then she had told us to write 'To Mom and Dad' on the packages after we had wrapped them.

"What are we going to make with milkweed pods and a hanger?" asked one boy.

"A wreath," the teacher replied. "Now, in other years your teachers helped you make your Christmas presents, but this year, you are going to make them all on your own. You're old enough to handle a project like this by yourselves."

"By ourselves?" another girl asked. "*All* by ourselves?"

The teacher smiled and nodded. "All by yourselves. First you will glue six milkweeds together so they look like poinsettias. When the flowers are finished, I will spray paint them either gold or silver for you, but then you can sprinkle them with glitter, if you want. Next you will stretch the wire hanger into a circle and cover it with butcher paper. You can leave the paper white, or you can sprinkle glitter on the paper, too. Then you will glue the flowers onto the paper. When everything is dry, you may also tie a bow around the top of the hanger, if you wish."

Poinsettias! My mother loved poinsettias. When it wasn't too cold outside, so that the plant wouldn't freeze while it was being carried from the car to the house, my big sister sometimes bought a poinsettia for Mom at Christmas.

Mom's last poinsettia had lived well into the summer, and for a while, she thought maybe it would make it until the next Christmas. But it didn't. Not after the curtain knocked it off the sewing machine cabinet one windy summer day and the pot had landed upside down on the floor, breaking off most of the leaves and stems and spilling dirt everywhere. My mother put the plant back into the pot, but it never recovered.

Finding a wire hanger for the poinsettia wreath that we were going to make would be easy. All of the closets at home, both upstairs and downstairs, had wire hangers. But where was I going to find milkweed pods?

I knew there wasn't any milkweed left around the edge of the barn-yard because one summer day Dad had used the scythe to 'make things look neater,' and when he had cut down the pigweed and nettles, he had also cut down the milkweed that was growing by the fence. The purple-pink milkweed flowers were a pretty color and smelled as sweet as any of the perfume my big sister dabbed on her wrists before she went to work—

Wait a minute.

What was that the teacher had said? That we were going to make the wreaths all by ourselves?

And right then and there, besides not having the foggiest notion of where I was going to find milkweed pods, I knew that I was in big trouble.

Art was my worst subject. I always followed the directions carefully, but no matter what we were doing—weaving Easter baskets out of long narrow strips of colored construction paper—making flower bouquets out of our traced hand prints—or painting black snow-covered trees on blue paper—my project always ended up looking as if I had made it with my eyes closed.

The Easter basket, for instance, had leaned so far to one side that it appeared as if a strong wind were trying to flatten it. The flower bouquet had resembled a fan made out of turkey feathers. And the snow-covered tree...well...in my opinion, the tree had looked more like a big black hairy spider with long dangling legs covered in a thick layer of white frosting.

The Christmas presents we made in other years had been different because the teachers did most of the work for us. Unlike other projects I had made in art class, I didn't have to worry about my Christmas present ending up crooked, so that when I gave it to my mother—

Uh-oh.

And that was another thing.

The wreath was going to be a present for Mom. And one of the rules about presents is that they are supposed to be a surprise.

So how was I going to sneak a wire hanger out of the house (and the milkweed pods, if I could find any), without my mother knowing?

A little while later the final bell rang.

Only one girl from my grade rode the same bus as me. She lived close to town and after she got off the bus and I didn't have anyone else my age to talk to, I had plenty of time to think about how to keep the milkweed pods and the hanger a secret so Mom wouldn't know we were making Christmas presents.

I was sure my mother wouldn't miss one hanger, but unless I could slip it under my coat without her seeing it, I was out of luck. It wasn't like I could just march out of the house on my way to school carrying a hanger without Mom wondering what I was up to.

As for the milkweed pods, even if I could find some, I wouldn't be able to cram that many into my coat pockets. But if I put the milkweed pods in a paper bag, then Mom would wonder why I was carrying a paper bag to school.

I finally concluded there was no way to keep the hanger and the milkweed pods a secret—although—after I had thought about it for a while—I realized that I didn't have to tell Mom what we were going to make. A hanger doesn't look like a wreath, and milkweed pods don't look like poinsettias.

Which brought me back to the first problem.

Where could I find some milkweed pods?

That night at supper, when Mom, Dad, my sister and I were all sitting at the table, I decided to just come right out and ask.

"Dad, do you know where there's any milkweed?"

My father frowned. "Milkweed? The last time I thought about milkweed was when I cleaned up around the edge of the barnyard, but—"

"What kind of a question is that?" my mother interrupted. "What do you mean, does Dad know where there's any milkweed."

"I, ahhh, well...I need milkweed pods for school."

"Milkweed pods? For school? To do what?" my mother replied.

"Ummmm...I...I can't tell you."

"You can't tell me?" Mom said, looking slightly perturbed. "Why on earth not?"

"It's...it's...going to be a surprise. I need a hanger, too."

"Milkweed pods and a hanger," Mom said.

"We're going to make presents," I explained. "In school. Together. The whole class."

"And that," Dad said, "is why she can't tell you what she needs them for."

"Because if you knew what they were for, it would spoil the surprise," my sister said.

"And presents have to be a surprise," my father added.

I flashed a grateful smile at Dad and Loretta.

"Do you know where there's some milkweed, then, Daddy?"

My father nodded. "Sure, by the ditch out toward the main road."

"Toward the main road?"

Dad grinned. "You went right past them when you were on the school bus, you know."

"Well," Mom said, "I can tell you one thing. It's too cold for you to walk that far—even if it is for school."

Our farm was about a half mile off the main road, but it wasn't much farther to the main road than it was to the far corner of the farm when I walked back to get the cows for milking during the summertime. And it wasn't cold. Even though the temperature stayed below freezing during the day, at night, it hadn't gotten down to zero yet, not like it would later on.

"But Mom—if I can't get any milkweeds..."

"Don't worry," my sister said, "we'll take the car."

The next morning, Loretta and I went looking for milkweed pods. We discovered a whole patch of them in the neighbor's pasture not far from the main road, right where Dad said they would be. There were enough for me, plus an extra thirty in case someone else needed them. The milkweeds were just on the other side of the fence, so we didn't have to struggle through the snow very far.

"What are you going to make out of milkweed pods?" Loretta asked as we put them into the paper bag we had brought with us.

After my sister promised to keep it a secret, I told her about the project.

"Oh," she said, "that sounds like it will be pretty."

Well of course it SOUNDED pretty. But since I was all thumbs when it came to art projects, the big question was—could I MAKE it pretty?

Two weeks later, after the nerve-wracking process of gluing the milkweed pods together so they would look like poinsettias—not to mention attaching the white paper to the hanger—never mind all of my attempts to glue the poinsettias onto the paper so they would stay where they belonged—as well as the many long minutes of trying to tie a length of red ribbon into an acceptable bow—the wreath was finally finished.

In the end, after the teacher had spray painted my poinsettias gold, I had decided to sprinkle both the poinsettias and the paper with gold glitter. The result reminded me of the way my bracelet sparkled in the sun. The bracelet was gold and had flowers all the way around it and a tiny '12k' stamped on the inside. My sister had given it to me for my birthday one year, and it was the only real bracelet I owned. I had a couple of other ones I had gotten at the fair that came to town every June, but they were made of thin plastic. I was only allowed to wear my real bracelet when I was dressed up for something special, like the Christmas program at church or at school.

Some of my classmates had used gold glitter on their wreaths, too, although most had decided upon red or green or silver.

"You should be very proud of yourselves," our teacher said, as she looked at the wreaths that were spread out on the library table and along the counter. "I think your mothers are going to be very proud of you, too."

It was then that I realized I had yet another problem.

How was I going to get the wreath home without ruining it so I could give it to Mom?

By some miracle—in spite of a crowded bus, a slippery driveway and a happy dog who was so glad to see me that he almost knocked me down—the wreath arrived home in one piece.

Other years I had waited until Christmas Eve to give Mom the present I had made in school. This year, I decided to give her my gift right away. I knew it would be risky to try wrapping the wreath (I didn't even want to think about gluing the poinsettias back on). And of course, if I waited until Christmas Eve, I would also have to figure out a way to take the wreath upstairs without my mother seeing it.

"You made a poinsettia wreath!" my mother said when I held it up for her inspection. "And it's even got a bow. And gold glitter."

"Are you surprised?" I asked.

She nodded. "I sure am. I had no idea you could do something like that with milkweed. Thank you!"

I laid the wreath on the table and then went to hang up my coat.

"Now," Mom said when I returned to the kitchen. "Where am I going to put it? Oh—I know. We'll take down the picture that's above the davenport so we can hang the wreath there."

And so we did.

Well, actually, I did, since Mom could not lean on the davenport for support and reach for the picture, all at the same time.

"Oh," Mom said, after I had hung the wreath, "doesn't it look pretty."

"You were really surprised?" I asked.

"Yes, I really was surprised," Mom said. "I tried to think of what you could be making with milkweed pods and a hanger, but I never considered it might be something like this."

When my sister came home from work, I immediately took her into the living room to show her what I had made.

"See?" she said. "Didn't I tell you it would be pretty?"

Even before Loretta had seen the wreath, I knew she would say she liked it. My big sister always said nice things about my art projects, including the snow-covered tree painted on blue paper.

A little while later, Dad came into the house after he had finished feeding the cows. As usual, he went into the living room to watch the news before we ate supper.

"Well, look at that," he said. "Loretta bought a wreath on her way home from work."

"Daaa-deeee! Loretta didn't buy it. I made it in school."

"Really?" he said.

My father bent closer to inspect the wreath. "So *that's* what you did with the milkweed pods."

He turned to me and winked. "I always knew milkweed had to be good for something besides keeping me in practice with the scythe. Although I don't know why I would have to stay in practice. Unless the hay mower breaks down. Or the combine. Then I guess I'd have to cut the hay and oats by hand like they used to do in the old days, wouldn't I."

Dad sat down on the davenport. "Was Ma surprised?"

I nodded. "She said she never knew you could make poinsettias out of milkweed pods."

But just then, I realized that Mom hadn't been the only one who was surprised. I had surprised myself too. In the first place, I had managed to find milkweed pods and to keep the whole project a secret, and now that the wreath was hanging on the wall above the davenport, it didn't look half bad.

Oh, sure, a couple of the poinsettias were a little crooked, but that was nothing compared to the lopsided Easter basket I had made.

Imagine that.

For once, I had finished an art project which didn't quite look as if I had made it with my eyes closed.

Almost maybe. But not quite.

****

~ 6 ~
Wintergreen

As we drove along the dirt road north of our farm one Sunday after-noon, the color of the sky reminded me of Mom's silver cream and sugar servers when they were tarnished and needed to be polished again.

Since morning, the sky had been cloudy, but now at mid-afternoon, the clouds had grown much thicker and darker. Earlier in December we had gotten a little snow. Several forty-degree days had melted most of it, and the landscape was a combination of dun-colored grass, black tree branches and the russet color of certain oak leaves.

Every year in December, Dad and I went on a Christmas tree expedition, and we were on our way now over to what we called our 'other place' to cut a tree. During the summer, I made frequent trips to the other place, a second farm my parents owned that was about a mile away, to help Dad with the haying or just to tag along when he checked on the corn or the oats or the soybeans.

But after school started, I rarely went to the other place, and it always took me by surprise how different it looked in the winter. Instead of green alfalfa and timothy and clover waving in a warm south breeze, what had grown back after third crop was now brown stubble that trembled in the face of a north wind. The fields were strangely silent now, too, without the songs of meadowlarks and bobolinks, and the bobwhite quail which lived in the narrow section of woods lining the road.

We were only about five minutes into our journey when Dad shifted the pickup truck down into first gear and then eased into the field driveway. The rutted track that ran along the edge of the hayfield was so bumpy that a merry jingling came from the glove compartment—probably a few bolts and washers, along with a couple of wrenches and maybe a screwdriver or two. When you're a farmer, you never know when you might need a wrench or a screwdriver or a bolt.

"Is it going to snow, Daddy?" I asked. Now that we had gotten past the trees lining the road, the sky had opened in front of us again.

Dad leaned forward to look up through the windshield.

"I'd say there's a pretty good chance," he replied.

"How much?"

My father shrugged. "Don't know. Maybe quite a bit. Wind's out of the east. And that usually means we'll get at least enough to shovel. Could be a lot more, though."

When we reached the pine plantation at the other end of the field, Dad turned the truck around, driving forward a few feet then backing up, then driving forward and then back again, forward and back, until we were facing in the direction we had come. He let the engine idle for a few seconds before shutting it off.

"Daddy?" I said, as we started walking toward the rows of planted red pine. "When do you think it will start to snow?"

Dad stopped and tipped his head back. "Soon," he said, "that wind feels raw and damp."

When my father said 'soon,' I was not expecting it to start snowing within the next ten minutes. At first, while we were cutting the tree we had selected, only a few random flakes drifted to the ground. By the time we reached the truck and had securely stowed our Christmas tree in the back, it was already snowing harder.

"If it keeps up like this all night, you won't have school tomorrow," Dad said as he started the truck. He slowly let out the clutch, and soon we were retracing our route along the field driveway. He turned on the windshield wipers, and with each pass—clickety-snick, clickety-snick— the wipers cleared an arc through the wet flakes plastered to the glass.

After we had pulled onto the dirt road, Dad shifted into second gear, although when we reached the "Y"—where you could either turn left to go toward our farm, or right to go toward the house that had at one time been part of our other place—he shifted into first gear again.

"Hope we make it up the hill," he said, glancing at me. "Wet snow makes the road kind of slick."

It was touch and go for a few seconds when the back wheels started spinning, but finally we reached the point where the hill leveled off. Trees grew on both sides of the road here, and to the right, a steep bank gave rise to a small wooded hillside.

"Look," Dad said, pointing toward the bank. He inched over to the side of the road and stopped.

I peered through the curtain of falling snow. The bank looked pretty much the same as it always had—exposed tree roots, patches of moss and bare spots where flat sandstone rocks had slid toward the road.

"What do you see?" I asked.

"Wintergreen," Dad answered. He shut off the truck and opened the door.

Wintergreen?

The first time I had tasted wintergreen, I decided that it was my favorite flavor. Peppermint was a little too sharp, although candy canes at Christmas were all right. Spearmint didn't taste like much of anything. Wintergreen, it seemed to me, was just right. In my opinion, Teaberry gum was the best, with wintergreen Lifesavers following as a close second.

Dad liked wintergreen too. Lifesaver books were popular gift exchanges at school for our Christmas party, and if the person who had drawn my name gave me a Lifesaver book, I would trade with other kids who had also gotten books. Sometimes I managed to acquire several extra rolls of wintergreen. Then I would share them with Dad. I thought Teaberry gum was better than candy because the taste lasted longer, but Dad preferred Lifesavers. Gum, he said, stuck to his dentures.

During the summer, every time I went to town with Dad to grind feed, I hoped he would buy a package of my favorite candy or gum. Not at the feed mill, of course. They didn't sell Teaberry gum or Lifesavers at the feed mill. But if we went to the restaurant for pie while we waited for our feed, or if Mom had asked Dad to pick up a couple of things at the grocery store, I would try to talk him into buying some gum or candy.

Going to the feed mill with Dad was a summertime activity, however, and there were long stretches during the school year when I never even saw a package of Teaberry gum or a roll of Lifesavers, much less had any in my possession.

So what was Dad talking about when he had stopped the truck and said, "wintergreen?"

I stared at the embankment and then at the hill beyond but I couldn't see anything out of the ordinary. I shut the truck door behind me just as Dad scrambled nimbly up the bank into the woods.

"It's growing all over here," he said, pointing to the ground. "They've got berries, too."

I struggled up the bank behind him to get a closer look. Underfoot were small plants with shiny green leaves.

"That green stuff is wintergreen?" I said.

My father nodded.

"Like what they use to make gum?"

"Yup. Here. Taste."

He reached down and picked a couple of small, pinkish-red berries, popping one into his mouth and handing one to me.

I sniffed the berry. It smelled like wintergreen, all right, but I wasn't one bit sure about eating the thing.

"Taste it," Dad urged. "You'll be surprised."

So, I ate the berry. It had a strange consistency—sort of dry and mushy, all at the same time…and then my mouth was filled with the marvelous taste of wintergreen. The same as my favorite gum, but different, too. More delicate.

"It's good!" I exclaimed, grinning. Then I frowned. "How come we haven't seen it before?"

"Usually too much snow by this time," Dad said.

"What about in the summer, though?"

"Too much underbrush and other green things."

"And this is really the stuff they use in gum?" I asked.

Dad took his cap off, slapped it against his leg to rid it of snow and then put it back on his head.

"Well…they probably don't go into the woods and pick wild wintergreen. People probably raise it and sell it, and I think they might use the leaves rather than the berries, but yes, this is the stuff."

By now the snow was falling so hard it made a hissing noise as it struck the copper-colored oak leaves above us. Unlike other trees, some of the oaks, I had noticed, keep their leaves until spring.

"How do you know so much about wintergreen?" I asked.

"Oh," Dad said, "when we were kids, we used to pick it so we could make ice cream."

I turned to look at him. "Ice cream?"

"Our kind of ice cream, anyway. A little dish of snow with winter-green berries mixed in."

Suddenly I struck upon a wonderful idea.

"I know! I can try some right now."

I took off my mitten, picked a few wintergreen berries and scooped a small handful of fluffy, fresh snow. I put the berries in the snow, and—well—I have to admit it was pretty tasty.

I put my mitten back on. "Didn't you have real ice cream when you were growing up, Dad?"

My father smiled. "Sure—sometimes. Not store bought, though. We made our own with a hand-cranked ice cream freezer. But that was mostly in the summertime. We thought wintergreen ice cream was an awful lot of fun."

Dad had been the middle child among several older brothers, an older sister, and three younger sisters. My grandparents had worked as cooks in a lumber camp in northern Wisconsin in the early 1900s. Many years ago, long before I was born, Dad had made his living cutting pulp wood.

"Daddy? How did you see the wintergreen from the road?" I asked.

My father hesitated before answering. "I didn't see it. Not today, at least."

I stopped trying to adjust my mitten so the thumb lined up like it was supposed to and turned my full attention toward Dad.

"Remember last fall, when the county forester came out here?" he asked.

"Yeah, I remember."

Just on the other side of the small wooded hill was a two-acre stand of tall red pine with a couple of rows of white pine next to the road. Dad said the trees were among the oldest of the plantations in the county that had been planted just after the Great Depression to keep the sandy soil from eroding. Nearly every year, the forester would come out to check on them. One year he used Dad's pine trees to demonstrate a brand new trimming device to foresters from other counties.

"Well," Dad continued, "while we were out here, I decided to take a little walk. I don't get much of a chance just to walk around back here."

"And that's when you saw the wintergreen?"

Dad nodded. "I was waiting for the right opportunity to show it to you."

He turned back toward the truck. "It'll be dark soon. We'd better get home. The cows are waiting to be milked."

As we slid down the embankment, I glanced over my shoulder.

Wintergreen.

Growing in the woods not far from my house.

And in that instant, I knew gum and candy would never again taste quite the same.

****

~ 7 ~
The Christmas Dress

From the time I was a very little girl, I had always loved to watch my big sister, Loretta, when she was sewing. So, one Sunday afternoon while she worked on the red velveteen jumper that was going to be my Christmas outfit, I didn't want to miss a single thing.

Because it was Sunday and Loretta did not have to go to work at the electric company, she was dressed casually in a white sweater and a pair of periwinkle blue slacks that matched her eyes. Loretta was an assistant bookkeeper at the electric cooperative that supplied electricity to our farm and to many of the rural areas in our county. I could still smell the perfume that she had worn when we went to church that morning. The bottle said it was called Lily of the Valley.

As Loretta spread the fabric on the kitchen table, I stood as close to her as possible, practically breathing down her neck.

When you live on a farm and the next-door neighbors are elderly and no other neighbors live on your mile-long stretch of road with children for you play with, and in fact, no other children live within several miles, what else is there to do on a Sunday afternoon in December except pester your big sister?

"What's this stuff for again?" I asked, taking a sheet of waxy paper out of an envelope.

"That's tracing paper," Loretta said. "I use it to make lines so I know where the seams should go."

I picked up the tracing wheel. "And that's what this is for, right?"

In a way, the tracing wheel reminded me of the spurs worn by all the cowboys in my favorite Westerns on television. I would have given almost anything to be a cowboy.

My sister glanced at me. She was busy pinning the pattern to the fabric.

"Yes. That's the tracing wheel."

I watched for a moment. "Can I help? Pleeeeease?"

Loretta smiled. "Sure. See how I've got the pins put in on this side? You can do the same on the other side."

I happily started pinning the pattern onto the fabric. The pins were the kind with little colored balls of plastic on the end: blue, green, white, yellow and red. Pinning the pattern was easy. Push the pin through the sheer pattern paper and the fabric, and then angle it to come out on top again. Push the pin through the fabric and angle it upwards. Push the pin, angle it up.

Everything went along just fine—for about the first six pins, anyway—until I bumped the pin container and knocked it onto the floor.

I never knew pins would scatter so far when they fell from the kitchen table and hit linoleum.

My sister looked at me, looked at the pins on the floor—and sighed.

After what seemed like a long time, we managed to retrieve all of the pins.

"I'll just finish this part," Loretta said. "It'll go faster that way."

Then it was time to cut out the pattern. As my sister expertly wielded the scissors, I couldn't help but think it looked like tremendous fun.

"Can I do that?"

She paused. "Ummmm—why don't you find the white tracing paper for me. That would be a big help."

I considered her suggestion.

"How come it has to be white?"

"Because it will show up better on this red fabric."

"But wouldn't blue be all right?"

I thought the blue paper was very pretty.

"No, the white is fine."

"Yellow?" I asked.

Loretta shook her head.

"Pink?"

"Just get out the white. That'll be the best."

I pulled the white tracing paper out of the envelope, and then, as Loretta continued to work, I kept right on asking questions: What happens if you don't pin the pattern? (It won't stay in place when you cut the fabric.) What's that funny scissors for? (A pinking shears; it keeps the

49

material from unraveling around the edges.) What are you going to do with the scraps? (Cover the buttons.) And on and on.

Finally Loretta was ready to sew the jumper. She moved into the living room to set up the sewing machine, and as she started to sew, I stood right by her elbow. Since this was going to be my dress, it seemed to me that I ought to keep an eye on the entire operation. And if I was going to keep an eye on things, then I had to ask more questions. Didn't I?

When Loretta had finished the first seam, she pulled the fabric back...and discovered that her finger was sewn to the dress.

I was horrified.

My mother was disgusted.

"I've been sitting here in the living room all afternoon, listening to you," Mom scolded. "It's no wonder your poor sister ended up sewing her finger to the dress. Your incessant talking is enough to drive anybody crazy."

Loretta finished snipping the thread. "No, no, it's nothing. See? Just a little bit of skin."

As I watched her pull the thread from her finger, my stomach did a small flip-flop.

"Maybe you'd better clean that up and put a bandage on it," Mom said.

A little while later, with a bandage securely wrapped around her finger, Loretta began to work on my dress again.

"How come...?" I said—and then I remembered that I shouldn't talk.

Loretta paused and looked over at me. "How come what?"

I shook my head. "Nothing."

I watched Loretta sew for a few minutes, and then another question popped into my head.

"What happens if..."

Loretta reached for the scissors and glanced over at me. "What happens if what?"

I shrugged. "Nothing."

Somehow I managed to make it through another five minutes without asking any questions.

After a while, Loretta looked over at me again.

"What's the matter?" she asked.

I shook my head.

"You're so quiet, I thought maybe something was wrong."

Loretta looked at me closely. "You're not mad at me, are you?"

I felt my eyes widen. "Mad at you? Why would I be mad at you?"

She shrugged. "You're never this quiet."

And without warning, tears filled my eyes. "I'm s-s-sorry I made you sew your finger. I didn't m-m-mean to…"

Loretta shook her head. "You didn't make me sew my finger."

"Yes, I did. Mom said."

"No, you didn't. I always thought it would happen someday. And today just happened to be the day."

For as long as I could remember, Loretta had been making clothes. Sometimes she sewed outfits for me, sometimes for herself, and sometimes for Mom. She even had a couple of skirts she kept in a trunk upstairs that she had made when she was in high school.

Loretta reached for the scissors again. "So, come on. Ask some more questions."

"Why?"

"Because it's not normal when you're this quiet. And besides, how are you ever going to learn about anything if you don't ask questions?"

In the end, Loretta finished the red velveteen jumper without further mishap. I wore the dress for the Christmas programs at school and at Sunday school, and for Christmas day, too, and for school when Christmas vacation was over.

But every time I put the dress on, I thought about Loretta's finger pierced with red thread. And about how she had said that it wasn't my fault when I knew, deep in my heart, that it was.

Maybe that's why I loved her so much. Not because she sewed clothes for me. And not because she wasn't angry when I spilled pins all over the floor or chattered non-stop when she was trying to concentrate.

But because, no matter what, I knew that my big sister always had time for me.

✳✳✳✳✳✳✳✳✳✳✳

~ 8 ~
White Christmas

After wearing a damp coat and stocking cap for the last hour, I felt chilled, and I was hoping the heavy wool blanket would help me warm up. We kept a blanket in the living room for just such a purpose, and this particular blanket had been issued to my brother when he served in the U.S. Army. That's what was stamped on the edge of the blanket: "U.S. Army."

"It's snowing," I announced to my mother as I sat down on the couch and reached for the olive-drab wool blanket to wrap around my shoulders.

The snow had started while we were milking. Every night after supper I went out to the barn with Dad. It was my job to carry milk to the milkhouse, and after the milker came off the last cow, it was my job to feed the calves. Once the calves had finished drinking their buckets of milk and the buckets had been rinsed and stacked, my chores were done. Dad still had to feed hay, but he said he didn't need my help to do that.

Each time I carried a bucket of milk to the milkhouse, when I returned to the barn, my coat and stocking cap were covered with a layer of snowflakes that began to melt as soon as I went back inside. On my way to the house, I had stopped for a minute to admire the fluffy feathery flakes as they fell from the black sky.

Across the room, my mother occupied the big easy chair next to the window where she always sat. The davenport, she said, was too low, which made it difficult for her to stand up.

"It's snowing?" Mom said, turning her attention away from the television to look at me. "Very hard?"

I shook my head. "It started when we were halfway through milking. There's maybe only about an inch on the ground so far."

"Well," she said, "I hope it doesn't snow too much. Dad and I are supposed to go Christmas shopping tomorrow afternoon."

My mother had never learned to drive, and after she had been stricken by polio sixteen years before I was born, the paralysis made it impossible for her to learn how. If she wanted to go somewhere, she always had to rely on Dad or my brother or my sister to take her.

"What time did the television show start?" I asked.

"Just a little while ago," Mom replied.

Every year a few weeks before the holidays when the Christmas specials began appearing on television, my mother liked to watch them after she had finished washing the supper dishes. The shows featured different entertainers who sang Christmas songs and performed elaborate dance routines with groups of pretty ladies wearing Santa hats and short red dresses trimmed with white fur.

To be honest, I preferred *Frosty the Snowman*, *Rudolph the Red-nosed Reindeer*, and Mr. Magoo's version of *A Christmas Carol*.

My mother turned her attention back to the television where a horse stood in front of a sleigh. I wondered how they had gotten the horse inside the building so he could pretend that he was taking people for a sleigh ride.

To me it seemed that bringing a horse into a television studio would be a little like bringing a horse into a house. Dusty, my brown pony with the white mane and tail, liked coming into the barn, but I could very well imagine that bringing her into the house would be a different story all together.

In the first place, Dusty would have to climb the porch steps, and after she made it up the steps, she would have to squeeze through the door into the house. If I asked her to do it, I knew she would probably oblige. I wasn't about to try it, though, because I was pretty sure that if I did, my mother would disown me.

The people on television really must have wanted everyone to think they were outdoors. As if the horse and sleigh weren't enough to make it seem like winter, they all wore coats and scarves and mittens and hats.

As the minutes ticked by, I discovered that many of the songs they performed were familiar to me, and when I knew the words, I sang along. Singing was fun. And Christmas meant that I had many opportunities to sing—at home with the television but also at school and at church while we spent hours practicing for our Christmas programs.

During the various songs, my mother occasionally glanced in my direction, but since she smiled and didn't seem to mind my off-key contributions, I continued.

Then another man appeared on the television screen. I didn't know the words to the song, although when the refrain came around again, I began to sing.

This time when my mother glanced at me, her eyes were filled with tears.

I abruptly stopped singing.

"What's the matter?" I asked.

My mother shook her head. "It's—no—it's nothing."

She reached for her crutches, pushed herself into a standing position and then slowly made her way toward the kitchen. I knew better than to follow right behind her. Mom became upset if someone followed her too closely because she said it made her feel like she was in the way and that she should hurry—except that she couldn't hurry.

A little while later, I went out to the kitchen and found my mother sitting by the table. She was crying.

"Mom? Are you all right?"

She put her hands over her face and leaned on her elbows.

I watched helplessly, not knowing what to do.

"Was my singing that bad?" I asked finally.

I couldn't think of anything else to say.

My mother didn't reply. After awhile she reached for a tissue and wiped her eyes. Then she smiled a little. "No, it wasn't your singing." She took a deep breath and let it out slowly. "It's that song. It always makes me cry."

"The song? What's wrong with it?" I asked.

"Oh," she replied, "there's nothing really wrong with it. In fact, it's a very pretty song. I just—hate it—that's all."

I stared at her, feeling a certain sense of shock.

Hearing my mother say she hated a song was a little like hearing her utter a swear word. Whenever I said I hated something, she would tell me I should say I 'intensely disliked' it, instead. Hate in any form, she insisted, was one of the evils in the world.

"You *hate* the song?" I asked.

My mother paused to gather her thoughts. "You know how it is when they release a new song and then they play it over and over again on the radio?"

Dad turned the radio on in the barn while we were doing the chores because he said it helped the cows to relax so they would let down their milk.

"Yes, Mom. I know. Sometimes we hear the same song three times while we're milking."

"Well, that's what happened with this one."

"So?" I said.

"So—that was the year I was in Madison," she explained. "When they were changing the wool packs, I would hear it. When I was in physical therapy, I would hear it. When they were washing my hair, I would hear it."

A few minutes later, with a tissue clutched in her hand, my mother began to tell me more of the story.

You see, the song was *White Christmas* and it had been released in 1942, the year my mother was stricken with polio. One November day, she felt as if she were coming down with a severe case of influenza, and her legs hurt so much she could barely walk out to the pasture to get the cows for milking. Not long after that, our house had been quarantined, and my mother found herself in the hospital in Madison, Wisconsin, flat on her back. She wasn't even allowed to have a pillow.

And while my mother was confined to that hospital bed two-hundred-and-fifty miles away from her family—her legs wasting away until they were all but useless—Christmas was going on without her. As the months came and went, she also missed her wedding anniversary. And the birthdays of my brother and sister who were three and five when she was taken to the hospital. The next time Mom saw them, they were four and six.

Eventually my mother learned to walk again by leaning her weight into the crutches and swinging her atrophied legs out from the hips, but it wasn't until May that she was well enough to go home.

As I sat in the kitchen with my mother, I thought about the words to the song and wondered what it would be like to be away from the farm for six months. To not see Mom and Dad, or Loretta and Ingman, or my dog, Needles, or my pony, Dusty. To know that Christmas was coming but that I wouldn't be here and that all I could do was imagine it in my dreams.

Mom reached for another tissue. "I suppose I shouldn't let a song bother me anymore after so many years, should I."

A few minutes later, Dad came into the house.

"What's the matter?" he asked as he hung his chore cap over the newel post.

"They played that song on television," my mother said. "You know, *White Christmas.* And it…well…it brought back so many memories. I guess I shouldn't let it bother me after all these years."

Dad shrugged as he unzipped his coat. "Nothing wrong with that. If it bothers you, it bothers you."

He paused before turning toward the bathroom. Dad always washed his hands and his face after he came in from the barn.

"You were gone an awfully long time," he said quietly. "I was afraid you would never be well enough to come home."

While my mother was in the hospital for six months, Dad, my brother and sister, and my maternal grandfather, Nils, had stayed on the farm. By that time, my maternal grandmother, Inga, was dead. In between doing the chores, Dad had cooked and cleaned and washed clothes and had taken care of his children and his father-in-law.

After Dad had left the kitchen to wash up, Mom reached for her crutches.

"Let's go back into the living room," she said. "At least they're done with *White Christmas* so I don't have to worry about hearing it again. Not tonight, anyway."

Maybe the television show was finished with *White Christmas*, but as I watched my mother make her way toward the living room, I suddenly realized that for her, it would never be over. That she would always move through life with halting, shambling steps, and could still only dream of those long-ago white Christmases—and of all the other things she used to know…

****

~ 9 ~
Good Things Come in Small Packages

For the last ten minutes, my big sister, Loretta, had been scrubbing the kitchen table. First she squirted yellow dish soap on the oilskin tablecloth, and then she went to work with a wet dish rag, moving it around in circles and back and forth and back and forth, making sure that she also reached all of the corners.

The dish soap smelled like lemons. That's what it said on the bottle. It had been a long time since my mother had made lemonade with fresh lemons, not since last summer, so I couldn't really remember if that's exactly the way lemons smelled.

When my sister finished scrubbing the table, she ran more warm water over the dish cloth, and then she began wiping off the soap.

Rinsing the table, it seemed to me, took more time than scrubbing it, even though the table wasn't dirty in the first place. How could it be? After our Sunday dinner of pot roast and carrots and mashed potatoes and coconut cream pie for dessert, as usual, the table had been cleared and thoroughly wiped.

Once my sister had finished cleaning the table for the second time in as many hours, she got out the big bowl she always used for mixing cookie dough and set it on the counter.

Even before Loretta took the bowl out of the cupboard, I knew how she intended to spend the afternoon.

When the kitchen table received an extra scrubbing on a Sunday afternoon in December, it meant only one thing: Christmas cookies.

Now the only question that remained was what kind of cookies?

Each year Loretta made a variety. Dozens of sugar cookies cut into shapes—stars, Christmas trees, bells, holly leaves, Santa Claus and reindeer that were frosted with pink or green or white or yellow or red icing.

My sister also made cookies with a date filling. And some little round ones called 'moth balls' which had walnuts in them and were rolled in powdered sugar.

Then, too, there were the rosettes. I found it fascinating that you could dip a piece of metal into batter and put it into hot oil and a little while later, out would come a golden brown, crispy rosette that looked like a snowflake.

And I mustn't forget the little round ones made out of coconut, powdered sugar and sweetened condensed milk that were dipped in chocolate, although the coconut balls weren't really cookies—they were more like candy.

By the time Loretta finished baking Christmas cookies every December, the big gold-colored tin canister with the red cover was full. For eleven months out of the year, the big canister stayed in the pantry and wasn't used for anything. But at Christmas, it was taken out every couple of days to fill the cookie jar that sat on the kitchen counter.

I always wondered how one family could eat so many cookies. My mother claimed that it was because I usually ate enough for three people.

"Don't eat too many of those. You'll get sick," she would say in an attempt to curb my appetite. Or, "If you keep eating those, you won't like cookies anymore." Or, "If you fill up on cookies now, you won't be hungry for supper."

And yet, I had noticed that my father ate his fair share of cookies, too, and I couldn't see that it had hurt him any. Dad said cookies helped him stay warm when he worked outside during the winter the same way a cob of corn every day helped my pony, Dusty, to stay warm.

After my sister got out the cookie bowl and set it on the cupboard, she rummaged around in the drawer until she found her favorite spoon—the stainless steel one with a wooden handle that had been a gift from our milk hauler. Every year the milk hauler left a gift for our family. Mom said it was 'a token of appreciation for our business.' Whatever that meant.

Besides the spoon, one year the milk hauler had given us a carving knife. Another year it had been one of those cheese-shaver-cake-or-pie-server things. I especially liked the spoon, however, since it played such an important part in baking cookies.

"What kind are you making?" I asked, as I sat down by the kitchen table to watch.

Sometimes Loretta started with my favorites—rolled sugar cookies. Not only were they covered with frosting, but they also were the biggest of all the cookies she baked. If Mom said I could have two cookies, I always picked the sugar cookies.

"I'm going to make spritz," Loretta replied.

This was one I had never heard of.

"Spritz? What's that?"

My sister reached into the cupboard and pulled out a box.

"I just bought this on Friday," she said.

When I had arrived home from school Friday afternoon, Dad was in the barn because one of our cows was having a calf. And of course, whenever there was a new a calf, I had to see it right away. And that meant I hadn't been in the house when Loretta came home from work, which explained why I hadn't seen the box before. My sister usually came home from working at Dunn County Electric around five o'clock.

Loretta opened the box and pulled out a device which looked a little like Dad's grease gun except that it didn't have a flexible hose for the grease fittings. A grease gun, Dad said, was an important piece of equipment on a farm. "If I don't keep my machinery greased, then I'll burn out bearings. And when I've got hay to bale or oats to combine or corn to pick, I can't afford to waste time on burned out bearings," he had explained after I used the grease gun one time to grease the hinges on my pony's stall door and had left it in the barn and he had spent an hour looking for it.

After the stall door incident, Dad had pointed out that oil would be better for hinges, so of course, I used the oil can the next time Dusty's door hinges squeaked. And then Dad had spent an hour looking for his oil can.

The grease gun and the oil can were just two of the reasons that my father constantly stressed the importance of putting things back where I had found them.

My sister held up the contraption she had brought home on Friday while I was out in the barn with Dad. "This is called a cookie press," she said.

"How does it work?" I asked.

"You pump the handle on top and it pushes the dough out of the bottom in different shapes," she explained.

Loretta reached into the box. "See?" she said, holding up a little round thing. "When we put this one on the bottom, it will make poinsettias."

It didn't exactly look like a poinsettia to me, but what did I know?

My sister unfolded a sheet of paper that was printed with the recipe and some instructions on how to use the cookie press.

A little while later, after Loretta had mixed the dough and had set it in the freezer for fifteen minutes to chill, she began filling the cookie press.

"Do the cookie sheets have to be greased?" I asked.

Putting shortening on the cookie sheets was ever so much fun. You got to use a little brush with a silver handle. It was sort of like painting.

Loretta shook her head. "With two sticks of butter in these things, they had better *not* stick to the cookie sheet."

My sister decided to try the poinsettias first.

The cookies came out in fat lumps and didn't look much like poinsettias.

Loretta frowned. "I don't think they're supposed to be like this. Maybe I should change the setting."

"Setting?"

"You can set it for thin, medium or thick," she explained, checking the recipe again. "Here it is. Says it's supposed to be on medium."

The next row of poinsettias came out looking much more like poinsettias.

"Can I try?" I asked.

Loretta handed over the cookie maker.

My poinsettias didn't look as good as Loretta's—but operating the cookie press was an awful lot of fun. More fun, even, than greasing the cookie sheets.

"Now we're going to sprinkle some of this on them," Loretta said, pointing to little bottles of red and green sugar crystals.

After the cookies had been in the oven for a few minutes, the scent of vanilla and butter began to fill the kitchen. It smelled so good, it was almost as if I could taste the air I was breathing.

When the first batch of cookies came out of the oven, Loretta used a pancake turner to transfer them to the table so they could cool off.

"They're so tiny!" I said, gazing at the rows of golden poinsettias colored with melted red and green sugar.

"Well, yes, they're tiny," Loretta said. "But that's the point. They're supposed to be a dainty cookie. Besides, haven't you ever heard the saying that good things come in small packages? Or look at it the other way. Bigger isn't always better."

As far as I was concerned, when you were talking about cookies, bigger was much better.

After a while, however, it dawned on me that smaller cookies might have distinct advantages. If four spritz cookies equaled one sugar cookie, then you could eat four times as many. Right?

Seemed like a good theory to me, anyhow—even if I never could convince my mother to see it that way.

****

Recipes for Loretta's Moth Ball Cookies, Chocolate Bonbons and Old-Fashioned Sugar Cookies are included in Appendix A.

~ 10 ~
Jeg Er Sa Glad Hver Julekveld

My mother heaved a deep sigh. "All right," she said. "Let's try it again."

For several weeks now, I had been working on learning how to sing *Jeg Er Sa Glad Hver Julekveld* (Yay Air Sa Glod Vair Yoola-kveld; just like it looks, of course.)

Fortunately, I knew the tune quite well: *I Am So Glad Each Christmas Eve*. It was singing the words in Norwegian that presented a much greater challenge. Especially since the only Norwegian I had ever heard spoken was the occasional saying uttered by my mother. Her favorite was, "if it wasn't stolen and it didn't burn up, it'll turn up someday." I didn't know how to say it in Norwegian myself although I ought to—I had heard it often enough.

My mother was born in Wisconsin in 1916, but both of her parents were immigrants from Norway. When Mom was a little girl, they spoke only Norwegian at home.

"Whose idea was this, anyway?" I grumbled as I looked at the Norwegian words my mother had written on a sheet of notepaper. Not that seeing the words helped me very much.

"Never mind whose idea it was," Mom said. "Please just try to learn the song, would you?"

Ever since my mother had informed me that I was going to sing *Jeg Er Sa Glad Hver Julekveld* as a solo for the Sunday school Christmas program, I had been walking around with butterflies in my stomach. I liked to sing, but to my way of thinking, there was a mighty big difference between singing in a group with the other kids and singing all by myself—in front of a whole church-full of people, too, no less.

If I could have heard Mom sing *Jeg Er Sa Glad Hver Julekveld*, it might have been easier to learn. But, as my mother claimed, she couldn't carry a tune in a tin bucket. And she was right. I had sat next to her church many times, so I knew she wasn't exaggerating when she said she couldn't sing.

"Let's try the first verse again," Mom said.

And so we did. And the second verse. And the third verse. And a repeat of the first verse.

"No, no," she said. "It's not 'ya' like you're saying 'yes.' It's 'yea' — but not like you're saying 'yippeeeee!'—it's got a shorter 'a' sound than that. And it's not 'sew' like with a needle and thread. It's 'sa.'"

She heaved another sigh. "At this rate, it'll be summer before you learn to sing it."

I briefly considered pointing out that a person could really get to hate *Jeg Er Sa Glad Hver Julekveld.* But then I decided it probably would be wiser not to.

By the time the night of the Christmas program arrived, my stomach felt like the butterflies had turned into caterpillars. Great big fuzzy ones that were squirming and crawling around. Up and down and back and forth. And up and down and back and forth.

"Just try to remember what I've told you," Mom said, right before the program started.

As if I could forget. We had only practiced the song about a hundred times.

"Who decided that I was supposed to sing all by myself?" I whispered.

My mother lifted one shoulder in a slight shrug. "The Sunday school superintendent," she replied in a low voice. "Lots of people around here have Norwegian blood, so she figured maybe they would enjoy hearing *Jeg Er Sa Glad Hver Julekveld.*"

Personally, I wasn't convinced that anyone would enjoy hearing me sing in Norwegian. Why would they? Other than Mom, I had never heard anyone else say a single word in that particular language.

I looked around at the inside of the little white country church. All of the pews were filled, with the exception of two toward the front. Only one elderly lady sat in the front pew.

Next to the piano stood a tall spruce tree decorated with colored lights, ornaments and tinsel. The spicy smell of the spruce needles mingled with the aroma of coffee brewing downstairs that would be served with lunch when the program was finished. Mom said I wasn't old enough to drink coffee, but that didn't stop me from appreciating the way it smelled.

A short while later when the Sunday school superintendent stood up to introduce the first class, the murmuring voices of the congregation grew silent. For fifteen or twenty minutes, the Christmas program went along uneventfully. Each of the Sunday school classes recited the Bible verses they had memorized and sang songs such as *Away in a Manger*, *Oh Little Town of Bethlehem, The First Noel* and *Oh Come All Ye Faithful*.

And then it was my turn.

On trembling legs, I walked to the front of the church and turned to face the audience. Before I had time to figure out whether I was in danger of fainting, the accompanist began playing the piano.

I drew a shaky breath.

"Jeg er sa glad hver jule-kveld, for da ble Jesus fodt. Da lyste stjernen som en sol, og engler sang sa sott."

When I reached the end of the first verse, I looked at the elderly lady in the front row. She sat only a few feet from me, and I could see tears trickling down the deeply etched lines in her face.

As I drew a deep breath and started on the second verse, the elderly lady wiped her eyes with a white handkerchief she had taken out of her purse, and then she smiled and nodded.

"Det little barn i Betlehem, han var en konge stor; som kom fra himlens hoye slott ned til var arme jord."

Somehow I made it through the third verse, too, and then a repeat of the first verse, and then another miracle occurred, because my shaky legs were carrying me back to my chair.

After the program was finished and we had gone downstairs to eat lunch (by which time my legs had finally stopped trembling), the elderly lady from the front row stopped to speak to me. When she smiled, her faded blue eyes lit up and small dimples appeared in her wrinkled cheeks. A jeweled brooch pinned to the front of her coat reminded me of the pin that my mother's aunt was wearing in a picture that Mom said had been taken in Norway.

Now that I was close to the elderly lady, I could smell her black wool coat. It gave off the faint aroma of moth balls, and it smelled just like my mother's 'good' coat did for the first half of every winter, until the moth ball scent faded away.

"My goodness, but I haven't heard that song in years. Mange takk… thank you," she said, reaching out to cup my chin with a hand that looked as though it had endured many years of hard physical labor. Then she leaned forward, put her arm around me and held me close to her for a moment.

'Mange takk' (pronounced 'munga tuck') was another phrase I had heard my mother use. It meant 'many thanks.'

"Mom taught me how to sing it," I explained.

"Oh," she said, "I should have known that Norma would have had something to do with it."

She smiled once again and then turned toward the kitchen where my mother was helping the other Ladies' Aid members serve lunch. A minute later, I overheard the elderly lady carrying on a conversation in Norwegian with my mother.

It was the first time that I had ever heard Mom speak Norwegian with someone. Even though I could not understand the words, my ears really perked up when I heard my name mentioned.

As it turned out, it wasn't until we arrived home later in the evening that I was able to ask my mother about it.

"What did that lady say?" I inquired as I unbuttoned my coat.

"What lady?" Mom replied, carefully lowering herself onto a kitchen chair so she could remove her snow boots. "There were a lot of ladies at church tonight."

"That lady who talked Norwegian with you," I said.

Mom bent forward to pull off one of her short black boots. "She said that hearing *Jeg Er Sa Glad Hver Julekveld* was the best Christmas present she's gotten in a long time. They used to sing it at home every Christmas Eve when she was a little girl."

"Why was she crying?" I asked.

My mother paused, looking startled. "She was crying?"

I nodded. "She cried the whole time I was singing. I even saw her take a handkerchief out of her purse so she could wipe her eyes."

As I slipped out of my coat, I wondered what it was about *Jeg Er Sa Glad Hver Julekveld* that made ladies cry because now Mom's eyes had tears in them.

"I am so proud of you," my mother said, holding out her arms.

I laid my coat on a chair and went over to her.

"I know you were scared to sing by yourself," she said, as her arms closed around me, "but I hope you realize what a wonderful gift you gave to a nice lady who has worked very hard all of her life."

I pulled back to look at her.

"There are so few of us around anymore who speak Norwegian," my mother continued, "so I suppose she thought she'd never hear another little girl sing that song."

"Another little girl?" I asked.

My mother nodded. "Another little girl like she was. She said you reminded her of herself."

I had a hard time picturing the elderly woman with gray hair and wrinkled cheeks as a little girl.

"Now aren't you glad that I taught you how to sing it?" Mom asked.

I still wasn't sure whether I was happy that I had learned to sing *Jeg Er Sa Glad Hver Julekveld*.

But I can tell you this.

Nothing would ever again make me sing it all by myself.

Not even a whole crowd of elderly Norwegian women who were as nice as the lady at church. Because just the thought of singing it again made my legs feel weak. And started the butterflies fluttering. And the caterpillars crawling.

On the other hand, I never thought anyone would like the song so much that it would make her cry. Or that she would say it was the best Christmas present she had gotten in a long time. Or that I would get a hug out of the deal.

Maybe learning how to sing *Jeg Er Sa Glad Hver Julekveld* wasn't that bad after all.

****

~ 11 ~
The Prettiest One Of All...

Dad stood by the kitchen door, waiting for me to finish getting ready to go with him. His coat was zipped all the way to the top, and he was wearing his red wool plaid cap and had the earflaps pulled down. His buckskin chopper mittens, the ones that had wool liners, were clutched loosely in one hand.

"Did you put on an extra pair of socks?" he asked.

I nodded.

"Good. You'd better take a scarf, too. And be sure to wear your chopper mittens."

I already knew that it was bitterly cold outside from my excursion to the barn earlier in the day.

"Is it colder than it was this morning?" I asked.

Dad shook his head. "It's not colder according to the thermometer, but the wind is blowing harder. Straight out of the north."

"Are you sure you should go?" my mother asked.

"Why not?" Dad replied. "As long as we're bundled up. Besides, Christmas is only a few weeks away so we've got to get a Christmas tree sometime."

"You could wait until tomorrow," my mother suggested. "Tomorrow is Sunday, so you'll have plenty of time in the afternoon."

Dad shrugged. "According to the weather forecast I heard on the radio in the barn, the wind is supposed to be as bad tomorrow, if not worse."

"Oh," Mom said. "Well, just be sure you get a nice one, then."

"Is there any other kind?" Dad asked.

He turned and winked at me. "We always get a nice Christmas tree, don't we?"

For as long as I could remember, Dad had said that finding a pretty Christmas tree was of the utmost importance. Once when I asked him why it was so important, he had replied, "we wouldn't want to have an ugly tree sitting in the middle of the living room, would we?"

And yet, Dad's answer didn't seem to quite tell the whole story. Even during the winter, farm work kept my father very busy. The task of cleaning the barn could turn out to be an all-day job, practically, if the tractor didn't want to start or if the barn cleaner and the manure spreader froze up.

And then, too, Dad had to feed the cows, do the milking, let the cows outside for a while so they could stretch their legs, wash the milkers, and on days when the milk hauler came to empty our new stainless steel bulk tank, he had to wash and sanitize the tank. He also chopped wood for the wood stove. And once a week, he took a truckload of corn and oats to town to grind feed.

Sometimes Dad also spent hours nursing one of our dairy cows through a difficult labor until at last the calf would be born. Then he spent more time drying the calf off with an old burlap feed sack, making sure the baby was close enough to its mother so she could lick it, and also making sure that when its legs were strong enough, the calf got a good dose of the mother's colostrum milk.

But none of the work that awaited Dad—with the exception of a cow and a newborn calf—was so important that it kept him from taking time to cut a Christmas tree. On a Saturday or a Sunday afternoon a few weeks before Christmas, Dad would announce that we were going out to cut a tree. And off we would go.

As Dad and I left the house, I pulled my scarf tighter so no cold air would seep in around my hood. To me, it seemed completely unfair that the sun could be shining so brightly while at the same time, the air made it feel like we lived in Alaska. We had just studied about Alaska in school, so I was sure that I understood exactly what the Eskimos went through every winter.

Ten minutes before we were ready to leave, Dad had started the truck to let it warm up. I was hoping that the inside of the pickup would feel as warm and comfortable as the living room when there was a roaring fire in the wood stove or when Mom thought it felt cold in the kitchen and she turned up the thermostat for the small liquid propane furnace located directly under the floor. A square grate occupied one corner of the kitchen, and when I came in from sledding and couldn't feel my toes or when Dad came in from spreading manure, his face purple with cold, we would pull up a chair to sit by the grate.

As we drove north along the dirt road toward our other place, the truck heater started doing such a good job of keeping me warm that suddenly, my eyelids began to feel droopy. I was afraid that if I let my eyes stay closed for too long, I might fall sound asleep.

"Well," Dad said when he finally brought the truck to halt not far from the pine plantation, "at least the sun is shining, so maybe it'll still be warm in here when we get back."

After I got out of the pickup and slammed the door shut, any notion that I'd had about feeling sleepy left as abruptly as a mouse eating oats in the granary when our dog, Needles, caught sight of it and gave chase. As we started walking toward the pine trees, even though we had only left the truck a few minutes ago, my fingers and toes were already beginning to feel numb.

"What about this little feller?" Dad asked, pointing to one of the smaller red pines. All of the trees planted on our farm were red pine. The trees we had for our classrooms at school were always red pine, too, although the Christmas trees we had at church were always spruce. One of the church members donated the trees from a plantation on his land.

I looked at the tree Dad pointed to and shook my head. Even though I would have liked to agree so we could get back into the truck and turn the heater on full blast, my conscience wouldn't let me.

"That's not a very good one. It's got a great big empty spot on this side," I said.

Dad shook his head. "Nope, we don't want that one, I guess."

We continued onward. Since there was so little snow on the ground, walking was easy, although the brisk north wind felt as if it were trying to slice the nose off my face.

"Can't hardly believe it got this cold so quick," Dad commented as we trudged along.

Neither could I. Last week it had been warm, with temperatures in the thirties and forties, but then, overnight, it had turned much colder and now it felt more like the end of January rather than the middle of December.

"How about this one?" I asked, pointing to another tree.

Dad inspected the red pine. Then he shook his head. "The trunk is crooked."

I stepped closer. About half way up, the trunk was bent at an angle that reminded me of the elbow in the pipe underneath the kitchen sink.

"How does a tree get a crooked trunk like that?" I asked.

Dad shrugged. "A deer probably bit off the top when the tree was small."

As we walked farther into the plantation, I heaved a deep sigh.

"Getting cold?" Dad asked.

"Maybe a little bit."

To be honest, it was more than a little, but I wasn't about to say so. Otherwise Dad might think we should go home. And I didn't want to go home. Not without a Christmas tree.

"I'm getting cold, too," Dad said. "The windchill must be way below zero."

Without warning, I began to cough. I couldn't help it. The cold, dry air put a tickle in my throat.

Dad stopped. "That's it. We're going back. It's just too cold out here. And I don't want you to get sick."

"But Daddy—"

"You wouldn't want to be sick on Christmas, would you?"

Without waiting for a reply, Dad turned around and headed back toward the truck.

Now here was a new development. It had never occurred to me that Dad would worry about me getting sick.

I hurried to catch up.

"But Daddy, Christmas isn't that far away and we need —"

I stopped abruptly and stared. Right in front of me was the most perfect tree. Somehow, we had missed it before.

"Daddy!"

My father stopped and turned around. If we hadn't almost walked past our Christmas tree, I would have been bothered by the scowl on his face.

"Look," I said, pointing.

Dad took a step closer. "Well, I'll be…"

He walked around the tree in one direction, and I walked around in the other. He looked at me and I looked at him. And then we both grinned.

"That's the one," Dad said.

While I steadied the trunk, my father knelt and, using the saw he had carried with him, cut the tree off about a foot above the ground.

"They're a lot easier to cut when there's no snow," he said.

I knew what he meant. Some years we had to bring a shovel with us so we could clear the snow away from the bottom of the tree.

Dad handed me the saw to carry, and then he picked up our Christmas tree and put it over his shoulder.

"Let's hope the truck is still warm," he said.

The inside of the truck felt much warmer than outside, but it wasn't until we reached the road that the heater started putting out plenty of heat again.

After we arrived home, we put our tree in the barn to thaw. Most years, the trees were covered with snow, and in the barn, the cows produced enough body heat so the temperature rarely dropped below freezing. This year, because it was so cold, Dad said it was even more important that the tree thaw first before we tried to bring it in through the kitchen door.

"When they're frozen like this, they're brittle, and it doesn't take much to snap off a branch," he explained, as he set the tree into a cement block turned on its side.

The cement block didn't hold the tree completely upright, but I knew it was better than leaning our Christmas tree against the barn wall because if we leaned it against the wall, when the tree finished thawing, one side would be flat.

Although it only took a few minutes to walk from the barn to the house, today, the cold wind made the distance seem more like a mile rather that just across the yard.

"I hope Ma's got the furnace turned up," Dad said as he opened the porch door.

We stopped in the porch to take off our coats and boots, and then we went inside. After being outside in that vicious wind, the kitchen felt as warm as a sunny summer day.

"Did you find a nice tree?" Mom asked.

Every year, my mother asked if we had found a nice tree.

And every year my father answered the same way.

Dad nodded as he held his hands over the furnace grate. "It'll be the prettiest one we've ever had," he declared.

"That's what you always say," Mom reminded him.

But you know what? My father was right. Even if the tree was less than perfect and we discovered a bare spot or some crooked branches that we hadn't noticed when it was still out in the pine plantation, once we had decorated it with lights, ornaments, tinsel and garland—and the tree stood in the living room by the picture window in the dusk of a late winter afternoon, shining for all the world to see—it really was the prettiest Christmas tree we'd ever had.

Until next year.

****

~ 12 ~
Better Yet...

My mother turned a stern gaze in my direction. "For the *last* time, I am NOT going to make sandbakelse," she declared.

Ever since Thanksgiving, I had been begging my mother to bake sandbakelse. Mom always started baking lefse after Thanksgiving, so I figured it would be a good idea for her to bake sandbakelse, too. Lefse and sandbakelse are both Norwegian, and since my mother was Norwegian (she was the daughter of Norwegian immigrants, wasn't she?), then why wouldn't she want to bake both sandbakelse and lefse?

Every year, sandbakelse ("sunbuckles") were served at lunch after our Sunday school Christmas program. In my opinion, the crunchy cookies shaped like little cups ranked right up there with cut-out sugar cookies frosted with colored icing.

Of course, the church ladies also served lefse after the Christmas program. And other kinds of Christmas cookies. And sandwiches. It almost goes without saying that Cheez-Whiz-and-crushed-potato-chips-on-nutbread were my favorite, although I liked the ham salad too. And let's not forget homemade dill pickles.

But the sandbakelse were extra special. I imagined that the little almond-flavored cookie cups would be even better filled with whipped cream.

On Sundays, we often collected cream from our milkhouse just before dinner was ready. My sister would whip the cream, and then we would eat it on apple or cherry or blueberry or blackberry pie for dessert. Since cream was so plentiful around our place, I knew that if I could only talk my mother into making sandbakelse, my vision of cookie cups filled with whipped cream could become a reality.

So I kept up my campaign.

Until one day, Mom had had enough.

"If you don't stop pestering me about those sandbakelse, I'm not going to make lefse, either," my mother said.

No lefse?

The prospect of a Christmas without lefse gave me pause for thought. Not for long, though.

"But why don't you want to make sandbakelse?" I asked.

Mom sighed. "Because," she said, "I don't have the patience for pressing the dough into the forms."

"What do the forms look like?"

"They're little metal cups that look just like sandbakelse. You have to take a lump of dough and mold it into the form with your fingers. And I simply don't have the patience to sit for hours and do that."

This did not seem like an especially good reason to me. My mother possessed plenty of patience when it came to embroidering flowers and leaves on dresser scarves and pillowcases. She would sit in her chair by the living room window and embroider for hours at a time. Sure, she said the embroidery was for a good cause because she gave most of it to the church to sell at the fall bazaar. As far as I could tell, giving the items to the church didn't mean she got done with them any faster.

My mother also possessed plenty of patience when it came to making lefse. I had never made lefse myself, although I could see that it took her a long time to roll out each piece of dough before she baked it.

"But Mom. You have lots of patience when you embroider. And when you make lefse. So why can't we have sandbakelse—"

My mother held up her index finger and then tapped it on the edge of the kitchen table for emphasis. "Not another word."

Even though once I had gotten an idea into my head and could be tenacious about it to the point of driving everyone else to distraction, when my mother tapped her finger on the table—I knew that was the end.

"Okay," I said, lapsing into a gloomy silence.

The silence stretched out over many minutes.

Finally my mother cleared her throat. "I don't like to make sandbakelse, but what if we make krumkake instead?"

"Kroom—what?" I asked.

"Krumkake."

"What's that?"

"They're crunchy, like a cookie. You bake them on an iron that has pretty designs in it, and then you roll them around a form so they end up looking like little ice cream cones when they cool off."

"Ice cream cones?"

Mom nodded. "Not the regular cones with a flat bottom, but the other ones. The waffle cones."

"What kind of word is that?" I asked. "Kroom…kaga."

"Norwegian," my mother replied.

I should have figured as much. With a name like 'kroomkaga,' it would have to be Norwegian.

The more I thought about it, however, the more that krumkake sounded like it might be fun. Maybe not as good as sandbakelse, but since I knew now that sandbakelse were completely out of the question, krumkake would have to be the next best thing.

"Could we really make some?" I said.

My mother smiled. "Yes. Except that I'll have to send your father to the store to see if he can find an iron. I don't have one."

Since the polio paralysis made it difficult for my mother to walk up and down store aisles, she often sent Dad on shopping errands. My father had even become pretty good at shopping for groceries. After Mom had made out her grocery list, he would go over it with her and would have her rewrite it so that the items were listed in the order that they appeared on the grocery store shelves. "That way I can go along the aisles and won't have to worry about missing anything. I can just work my way down the list," he'd say.

In preparation for a trip to the grocery store, Dad would put on a clean blue chambray work shirt, clean overalls, and would wear the new blue-and-white pin-striped chore cap that he kept 'for good.' Other farmers, I had noticed, weren't quite so thoughtful. As soon as we walked into the store, I could tell immediately if there was a farmer who had come straight from the barn. The smell of cow manure and silage that clung to their boots and clothes always gave them away. Dad said that if he didn't change his clothes first, the barn smell would make the prospect of buying food so unappetizing that he wouldn't feel like being in the grocery store.

Seeing as my father was so good at shopping for groceries, I figured he ought to be equally as good at shopping for a krumkake iron.

"Could we make krumkake this weekend?" I asked.

"If Dad can find an iron," Mom replied. "I haven't made it in years. My mother used to have an iron. I'm not sure what happened to it, though."

As luck would have it, Dad was able to find a krumkake iron. But only after he had visited every hardware store within twenty miles.

"It looks like a waffle iron," I said a few days later as I examined the purchase Dad had made.

"Well, yes, it does," Mom replied. "Krumkake look like little thin waffles before they're rolled up."

My mother reached for the box and then frowned. She held up a metal cone.

"Uh-oh."

"What's wrong?"

"This is not good."

I looked at the cone. "Why not?"

"Because when you roll the hot krumkake onto it, the cone gets hot and then you burn your fingers."

Wouldn't you just know it. Krumkake was almost within my grasp—and now this…

"So," Mom continued, "what we need is a clothespin."

"A clothespin?"

"Yes, go down to the basement and get a couple. Not the pinchy kind but the other ones. I think we still have a few of those left."

During the summer when my mother hung clothes outside to dry, she liked to use the 'pinchy' clothespins because she said they kept the clothes on the line better if it was windy. I went down to the basement and discovered that Mom was right. We did have a few of the other ones left. I brought three of them upstairs. My mother washed them in hot, soapy water and then set them on a clean dishtowel to dry.

The next Saturday afternoon, Mom and I made krumkake. My mother used the recipe that came with the krumkake iron, and I was surprised to see that the batter was so thin. Because the krumkake iron looked like a waffle iron, I guess I expected the batter to be thick like waffle batter.

When the krumkake came out of the iron, they were only a shade or two darker than butter. Mom baked them, and it was my job to roll them onto a clothespin and then to slip them off the clothespin once they were cool.

Each krumkake was covered with a swirled pattern that reminded me of the lace on the bottom of our kitchen curtains. They almost looked too pretty to eat, but I was afraid to say so. I didn't want Mom to get any ideas.

When we had baked a half a dozen, my mother suggested it was time for 'taste testing.'

"Mom!" I exclaimed after I had taken my first bite. "These are GOOD!"

The little cookie cones were crunchy and sweet and tasted of vanilla.

My mother smiled and reached for another krumkake. "Yes, they are good. I had forgotten just how good."

Well, all right. So maybe I wasn't going to have sandbakelse filled with whipped cream. But all of a sudden I realized that it didn't matter. Krumkake would be even better.

And so it was.

****

~ 13 ~
The Most Perfect Toboggan

One December afternoon as I trudged up the driveway from the school bus, I figured it was time to take my sled out of the garage and put it to good use. Six inches of beautiful, white fluffy snow covered the ground, and it had arrived just right, too, over a couple of different snowfalls, so that by now, the driveway was perfect for sledding.

I quickly changed out of my school clothes, grabbed a couple of cookies, and then I was on my way. I hadn't had a chance to go sliding since last winter, and traveling at top speed, with the sled's metal runners cutting narrow lines through the packed snow, was every bit as much fun as I remembered.

After a while, I lost count of the number of trips down the driveway. The sun sank below the horizon, and I knew that it would soon be dark.

As I reached the top of the driveway and turned around to make one last trip, headlights came over the hill closest to the church. Since cars hardly ever traveled our road, especially during the winter, I waited to find out if it would stop at the neighbor's place, if it would turn into our driveway, or if it would go on by.

When the vehicle drew closer, I could tell it was the veterinarian's truck. One of our cows had been lame last night, so if the vet was coming, her foot must have been worse today. A little while later, the truck turned into our driveway. The vet grinned and waved as he passed by me. I waved back, and then I hopped on my sled for one last glorious ride.

By the time I had put my sled away and had gone back into the house, I had forgotten all about the vet.

My mother had not.

She just happened to be looking out the kitchen window when he drove in, and as far as she was concerned, it had been a 'close call.'

"I should have remembered, too. But I didn't," she said. "It was getting so late, though, I guess I thought he might not come until after supper."

"But Mom," I said, as I took off my boots, "I saw the truck. That's why I waited."

My mother put a cover on the pan of boiling potatoes, and it seemed to me that it crashed down with just a little more force than necessary.

"I don't care," she said, turning around to reach for the edge of the table so she could sit down. "That's exactly the kind of thing I've been worried about. You know I don't like it that you go all the way into the road with your sled. It would only take one car at the wrong time, and, well, I don't like to think about what could happen. After this, I want you to slide in the pasture. And I don't want any arguments about it."

"But—"

My mother shook her head. "Not another word, young lady."

"But Mom. The only time anybody drives on our road is the milk truck, and he comes in the morning. And it's just the school bus in the afternoon. And I'm riding on the bus, so when it's gone…"

The look on my mother's face convinced me that perhaps I should stop while I was ahead.

The hill that formed our driveway also formed the north side of the pasture. An even steeper hill made up the south side, and at the bottom of the two hills, a narrow, flat area parallel to the driveway drained toward the creek situated next to the road.

I had tried sliding in the pasture before, but, to be honest, it wasn't much fun. Of all the frustrations which came along in my life, pitching forward to land face down when my sled came to abrupt halt ranked right at the top. Tufts of long pasture grass and the occasional gopher mound hidden by the snow did not create ideal sledding conditions.

As I took the plates out of the cupboard and began setting the table, I tried to think of some way to convince Mom that it would be better for me to slide on the driveway.

After the veterinarian had left and Dad and Ingman had come into the house and we were all sitting at the table (except for my sister; she had already moved into an apartment in the town where she worked so she wouldn't have to drive back and forth every day on slippery roads), I began my campaign.

"Daddy? What do you think is safer—sliding down the driveway or sliding in the pasture."

Dad glanced across the table at my mother. "Well...ahhh...errr...I don't know. Haven't really thought about it."

"Mom says the pasture is safer, but I think the driveway is better."

"The driveway is *not* better," my mother interrupted. "Why, the vet almost ran over you tonight."

Dad abruptly set down his fork, pushed back his chair, and reached for his handkerchief. Instead of wiping his nose, the white handkerchief was really hiding a smile. Mom sat directly across from him, though, so she wouldn't know that.

My father vigorously wiped the end of his nose and then stuffed the handkerchief back into his pocket.

"Now Ma," he said, as he moved his chair closer to the table and picked up his fork again, "the vet did not almost run over her."

"How would you know?" she asked indignantly. "I saw the whole thing from the kitchen window."

Dad shook his head. "I saw the whole thing, too. When I noticed the headlights while I was feeding hay, I was hoping it was the vet, so I stood outside by the barn door. She wasn't even on her sled."

"Hmmmphhh!!" Mom replied. "What did you see, Ingman?"

My brother picked up his knife so he could cut a chunk of roast beef into bite-sized pieces. "I didn't see anything," he said. "I was feeding hay on the other side of the barn."

"Oh," Mom said.

I took advantage of the pause in conversation to point out all of the problems with sliding in the pasture. The gopher mounds. The tufts of long grass. The barb wire fence. The creek at the far end too.

"So, Daddy," I concluded, "wouldn't the driveway be better?"

My father looked at me for several moments and then reached for the bowl of green beans and ladled two heaping spoonfuls onto his plate.

"What you need," he said as he set the bowl of green beans in the middle of the table and then reached for the butter, "is a toboggan. You won't pick up enough speed coming down the south side to make it to the fence by the driveway. The hill's not long enough."

"But what about using my sled on the driveway?" I asked.

Dad shrugged. "Your sled doesn't work very well in the pasture. But a toboggan would. You've got enough sense not to start down the driveway if there's a car coming from the south, but if a car came from the north, that would be a different story because you wouldn't be able to see it."

I had never thought about a car coming from the other direction. The sloping field east of the house—and the trees at the bottom of the hill—blocked the view of the road to the north.

I had never thought about owning a toboggan, either. Now that Dad mentioned it, maybe I did need one. A couple of my friends at school had toboggans and they said they were tons of fun.

Dad reached for the plate of sliced homemade Christmas bread. During December, Mom would make several batches of Christmas bread.

"So, is that what you'd like for Christmas? A toboggan?" he asked as he began buttering a slice of bread.

I thought about it for a few moments. If I had a toboggan, I could go sliding in the pasture any time I wanted to and wouldn't have to keep talking Mom into letting me use the driveway.

"A toboggan? For Christmas? Could I?"

On the other side of the table, my mother frowned and held up her hand.

"Now hold on. There's absolutely nothing wrong with your sled. And one little girl doesn't need a great big toboggan. Besides, you'd get tired of dragging a toboggan up the hill and then you wouldn't want to play with it anymore."

I gave my mother a cool, hard stare. Little? What did she mean by that? I wasn't a 'little girl' anymore. The kindergarten kids were 'little girls.'

Ingman coughed and almost choked on a mouthful of milk. "Ha-ha," he spluttered. "She wouldn't get tired of dragging a toboggan. She'd take Dusty out there and make her pull the toboggan up the hill."

Dad grinned, and I knew he was imagining my plump little brown pony with a toboggan tied to her white tail. Although, now that I considered it, maybe it wouldn't be such a bad idea…

"No, no," Ingman said hastily. "You wouldn't want Dusty to pull a toboggan. She might get her feet tangled up in the rope."

I turned to my mother. "Could I get a toboggan for Christmas? Please? Pretty please?"

For a few seconds, I thought maybe she was going to come around.

But then Mom shook her head. "Don't get your hopes up."

My anticipation evaporated instantly. When my mother said 'don't get your hopes up,' it was as bad as when she said 'we'll see,' because they both usually meant 'no.'

Then Dad caught my eye and winked, and I knew—somehow—he would convince Mom that a toboggan should be under the tree at Christmas.

As they did every year, when Mom and Loretta started wrapping Christmas gifts, they stowed them in the upstairs and downstairs closets. And as was the case every year from the beginning of December until Christmas, I was forbidden to open any of the closet doors. If I needed something, Mom or Loretta would get it for me.

But that didn't stop me from stealing peeks when one of *them* opened a closet door. Every chance I got when I knew Mom or Loretta was headed for a closet, I tried to be somewhere close by. From a variety of vantage points, I managed to catch glimpses of round packages and flat packages, small square boxes and larger square boxes. There was even one package that appeared to be a bottle (bubble bath?).

After two weeks of surreptitious reconnaissance missions, however, I hadn't glimpsed any presents that were big enough to be my toboggan.

Then one Sunday evening as Loretta was getting ready to go back to her apartment she opened the upstairs closet to find a sweater, and the answer was so obvious, I felt like banging my head against the wall. Of course a toboggan would be much too large to keep in the house. And if the toboggan was too big to be kept in the house, then it had to be hidden outside.

The next day after school, I started my investigation of the outside buildings. I told my mother I was going to see Dusty (which I did), but then I took a few extra minutes to check the machine shed, the garage, the granary and the corn crib.

No toboggan.

I wasn't especially worried, though. After all, my father had winked, so I was sure the toboggan would show up underneath the tree by the time we opened our gifts. Mom and Loretta always waited until Christmas Eve to put the presents under the tree while I was in the barn with Dad and Ingman during milking.

To satisfy my own curiosity, as Christmas drew closer, I maintained my vigil when the closet doors were opened. And I continued to sneak into the other farm buildings during spare moments.

Still no toboggan.

Yet.

Finally Christmas Eve arrived.

While I fed the calves and scraped down manure from behind the cows and fluffed bedding and helped feed hay, I tried to decide which was going to be more fun: finding out where the toboggan had been hidden, or seeing how Mom and Loretta would put something that big underneath the tree. Then again, maybe the toboggan wouldn't be under the Christmas tree. Maybe it would be standing up in the corner. Either way, I hoped the toboggan would be wrapped in colored paper, although, even if it wasn't, that would be all right, too.

When the chores were done and the whole family had gathered in the living room, it only took me a moment to notice all of the packages under the tree were of a completely ordinary size. I quickly glanced at all four corners of the room. No toboggan leaned against the wall, either.

I suddenly felt as if the floor had dropped away from beneath my feet. I had been so sure about the toboggan that I had never once lost faith it had to be hidden somewhere. But now I could see that I was wrong. As wrong as I had ever been about anything.

While the rest of the family laughed and chatted and exclaimed over their presents, I went through the motions of opening my gifts and thanking the person who had given it to me. Mom said it was important to say thank you and that people who forgot to say thank you didn't deserve to get presents.

As it turned out, the bottle-shaped package was bubble bath, although I was pretty sure that Dad had not purchased it himself. I opened the bottle and breathed deeply. An image of the big lilac bushes in our backyard heavy with blooms on a warm May evening flashed before my mind's eye. Then it was gone. I put the cover back on the bottle and decided that even bubble bath couldn't make me feel better about the toboggan.

"Thank you, Daddy," I said quietly.

"What's the matter?" Dad asked. "Don't you like it? I told Loretta to get lilac because it was the prettiest flower I could think of."

Just then, I noticed Dad was wearing what my mother called his 'cat that swallowed the canary' smile. Usually the smile meant he was really pleased about something, although I didn't think lilac bubble bath was worth feeling all that pleased with himself.

"Oh, yes, Daddy. I like it. It makes me think about spring and going out with you to see the lilacs at night after milking."

Dad nodded in satisfied way, reached for his pocket knife, and began cutting the tape on a gift that Loretta had just handed to him.

After what seemed like a very long time, no more presents were left under the tree. When the final piece of wrapping paper had been stuffed into a paper grocery bag, I figured maybe now I could forget about the toboggan. Mom had warned me that I shouldn't get my hopes up, but I had done it anyway. And maybe, too, I could forget about all the time I had wasted trying to peek into closets and sneaking in and out of buildings—

"Say!" Ingman exclaimed, turning toward me. "What's that underneath Mom and Dad's bed?"

My parents' bedroom was just off the living room, but I wondered how Ingman could see anything from where he was sitting. My brother occupied one of the end of the couch and Dad sat on the other end.

"Maybe you should go look," Dad suggested.

I noticed that my father was once again wearing his cat-that-swallowed-the-canary smile.

"Yes," chimed in Mom and Loretta. "See what it is."

I didn't especially feel like crawling around on the floor to look under the bed. Not after what I'd just been through. What I really felt like doing was putting on my pajamas and going to sleep.

I turned to look at Dad, Ingman, Mom and Loretta. They were all watching me with expectant expressions.

I went into the bedroom and got down on my knees. It was really dark under the bed...but...I could just make out a large, flat package.

"Need help?" Ingman asked.

I looked up at him in mute appeal.

He grinned and knelt down beside me. His muscular arm disappeared under the bed and a few seconds later, the package came into view.

Could it be?

No. It couldn't.

It was much too small to be a toboggan.

Ingman carried the package into the living room, set it on the floor and stood back. The package was covered in wrapping paper, but the corners looked as if someone had hastily crumpled the paper together, folded it over, and then had slapped on tape to hold the corners.

"Well," my brother said as I looked down at the package, "aren't you going to open it?"

When I had torn away the first handful of wrapping paper, I could see alternating strips of red paint and varnished wood.

I tore away another handful of paper—and—YES!—it WAS a toboggan!

But it was like no toboggan I had ever seen. Instead of very long with a large, curled over front, it was much smaller with only a slightly curved front.

Sort of just my size, in fact.

I looked at my mother, father, sister and brother.

"Dad told me about a boy he knew when he was growing up who lost a finger when his brother accidentally ran over his hand. Quite honestly, I never thought that a sled's runners might be that sharp," Mom said.

I glanced at Dad, who favored me with the briefest of winks.

"So," Mom continued, "we thought a small toboggan would be better for you than a great big one. Easier to steer by yourself since you'll usually be the only one on it."

"Did you go shopping for it?" I asked Loretta. She was the logical choice, since she stayed in town all week. And yet, I wondered how she could have brought it into the house without me noticing.

My sister shook her head. "No, I didn't shop for it. Dad did."

I turned to my father. "You went shopping?"

Dad thought of wonderful ideas for presents (like lilac bubble bath), but he never went Christmas shopping. That was Mom and Loretta's job.

"Got it while you were at school, on the last day before vacation," he explained.

"Dad and I wrapped it," Ingman said.

I turned to stare at my big brother. *"You* and *Dad* wrapped it?"

My mother cleared her throat. "Excuse me, but I helped, too, you know. Although, I guess what I mostly did was hand out pieces of tape."

If Dad and Ingman wrapped it—and Mom, who was notoriously hopeless at wrapping gifts, had supervised—no wonder the corners had been crumpled and lopsided.

"Did we surprise you?" Mom asked. "We tried really hard to keep it a secret."

"We thought about putting it outside someplace, because Ma was afraid that you'd look under the bed," Dad said.

"But then, by the time we got it wrapped, we looked out the window and saw the school bus coming," Ingman explained.

"So putting it under the bed was the best we could do. You *are* surprised, aren't you?" Mom asked.

Surprised? Of course I was surprised.

Because what kind of a dirty rotten trick was that anyway? Finding the most perfect little toboggan—and then hiding it in a place I had never even thought to look?

****

~ 14 ~
Christmas Tree Surprise

We were in a quandary over the lack of suitable Christmas trees. That's what Mom said. Dad said it was a dilemma. Either way, it meant that we didn't have any Christmas trees. We had always cut a tree from one of the pine plantations on our farm, but this year, all of our older trees were too big to bring into the house, and the ones that had just been planted only a few years ago were still too small.

Last year, Dad had cut one of the middle-sized trees in half so that we could use the top part, but then over the summer, the trees had grown a foot or two, and Dad said he didn't want to leave another half a tree in the plantation.

Mom said she didn't see anything wrong with leaving half a tree when it was going to be used for Christmas. Dad said it was one thing to cut a small tree, because that would leave more room for the others to grow, but that it was quite another to waste half of a larger tree, especially one well on its way to being fencepost size. Mom said she had forgotten about the fenceposts.

My big sister, Loretta, wondered if anyone who lived nearby had trees that were the right size. Dad said he couldn't think of anyone, but Mom said even if he did, she would rather not ask someone else if we could cut a Christmas tree from their property.

As I listened to Mom, Dad and Loretta discuss the shortage of Christmas trees, I felt a growing sense of alarm. Since we had always cut a tree from our farm—and since we did not have any trees this year that were the right size—did that mean we would not be able to have Christmas? I wasn't sure if you could have Christmas without a tree, but even if you could, well...it just wouldn't be the same.

Then one Friday evening, my sister made an announcement.

"I have an idea for a Christmas tree," she said after we had sat down to eat supper.

"What's that?" Dad asked, reaching for the bowl of mashed potatoes.

"I don't want a jack pine," my mother said.

"Why not?" I inquired.

Jack pine grew on the west side of the big wooded hill behind the barn that we called The Bluff. Dad said he liked jack pine because they were tough. If heavy wet snow fell in late winter or early spring, other trees would break off, but jack pine would just bend under the weight and wouldn't break.

I thought jack pine were pretty because they were all so different. In school we had learned that no two snowflakes are the same, and it seemed to me jack pine were like that. Some were tall and narrow. Some were short and fat. And some were covered with branches only on one side if another tree, a pin oak or a white oak, grew too close.

Another thing I liked about jack pine was the way they smelled. In the heat of a summer's day, jack pine pitch smelled so good, I wished that I could put it in a jar. I wasn't sure what I would do with the jar. Keep it on my dresser, maybe, so that in the middle of the winter, when it was twenty degrees below zero outside and too cold to go sledding or to ride my pony, Dusty—or so cold that my feet hurt when I was carrying milk to the milkhouse—I could open it and smell the pitch and think about how much fun I would have when summer arrived once again.

"Years ago when we didn't have any other kind of trees, we always had a jack pine," my mother said. "I don't want another one of those ugly things in the house."

"Jack pine aren't ugly," I protested.

"Yes they are," Mom replied.

"No they're not. Daddy says they're tough."

"I don't want one in the house," Mom insisted.

"What's your idea for a Christmas tree?" Dad asked my sister.

"It will be a surprise," she said, turning to me. "You and I will find one."

I felt my eyebrows creeping up on my forehead. "We will? Where?"

"Right here on the farm."

"But we don't have any trees," I said. "Not ones that we can use for Christmas."

"Yes, we do," Loretta replied. "Wait and see."

"Just as long as it's not a jack pine," Mom said.

"It won't be a jack pine," my sister assured her.

The next afternoon, Loretta and I set out for the back of the farm. Christmas was two weeks away, but so far, we had only gotten a couple of inches of snow, just enough to remind me that it was almost Christmas. The air smelled clean, the way that clothes smell clean after they have been hung outside to dry, and the only sounds I could hear were some crows cawing and a distant train whistle. We couldn't see the train tracks from our farm, although we could hear the whistle from a long ways off when the trains approached the crossings.

"But Loretta, we've only got big trees back here," I protested as we walked along the lane. The sun was shining, and while it wasn't exactly warm outside, it wasn't really cold. To our right was The Bluff and to our left was one of the alfalfa fields where we baled hay during the summer.

"I know there's only big trees back here," Loretta said. "But we're going to get a Christmas tree, anyway."

"How?"

"By climbing one of the great, big trees," she said, holding up the saw she had brought, "and cutting off the top."

I thought about the idea for a little while.

After the polio, the doctors had told Mom she would never have any more children, so when my mother said I had been a 'surprise,' she really meant it. Loretta is almost twenty years older than me, and she was the most glamorous woman I knew. When she was on her way to church or to the office where she worked, her slim figure was dressed in pretty outfits and high heels, with necklaces and earrings to match, her dark curly hair arranged just so, and wearing rosy lipstick that was the same shade as her fingernail polish. Sometimes she even put on a hat and gloves. My favorite dress was half black and half white on the top with the skirt black and white on opposite sides. I liked the sea-green two-piece suit too. And then there was the dark blue wool skirt with the light blue blouse. No matter what Loretta wore, though, she always looked like a movie star to me. Even today, in an old pair of corduroy slacks and an old sweater, she was still the prettiest woman I knew.

And now my glamorous big sister was going to climb a tree? Without a ladder? To cut off the top?

"But," I sputtered, "how are we going to get up there?"

"You'll see," Loretta replied.

Finally we arrived at the back of the farm where the largest trees grew. They were all red pine, their green branches made up of long two-needled clusters. The trees were so tall, to me they looked like they almost touched the clear blue sky.

As we walked along the outside row, we carefully studied each tree, and I had to keep reminding myself that we didn't need the whole tree, just the very top.

"What about that one?" I asked after a while, pointing to a tree that seemed to stand out a little from its neighbors.

My sister walked around to one side and then to the other.

"Looks good," she said.

Before I quite knew what was happening, Loretta was halfway to the top, using the branches that grew out of the trunk at ninety degree angles to pull herself up. I didn't want to be left behind, so I climbed the opposite side.

"I think we're high enough," Loretta said a few minutes later as she struggled to put the saw into position.

I looked down at the ground. From here, the tree seemed even taller yet.

"How are we going to get it down after you cut off the top?" I asked, as I hooked my arm around a branch to steady myself.

"That's where you come in," Loretta explained while she began sawing. "When I have it almost cut through, I'll say 'now' and then you push so it falls away from us."

For a few minutes, the only sound was the rasping of the saw as it cut into the trunk and the whispering sigh of a light breeze as it rustled the pine boughs around us.

"Now," Loretta said.

While she finished sawing the last little bit, I started pushing. With a whoosh and a plop, our Christmas tree landed on the snow-covered ground below.

"We did it!" I yelled.

"Well, not quite," Loretta said, now able to look directly across at me without the treetop between us. "We still have to get down yet."

A few minutes later, we were both safely on the ground.

"You grab the bottom branch on that side, and I'll take the one on this side," Loretta said.

The tree was not as heavy as I thought it might be, and together, with a few rest stops along the way, we managed to drag it all the way back to the house.

"Where on earth did you find one?" Mom asked, when we walked into the kitchen a little while later. She was standing in front of the west window, looking out at our Christmas tree.

Loretta explained.

Mom turned toward us and shook her head. "You girls should not have been climbing such a big tree," she scolded. "What if you had gotten hurt?"

"Now, Ma," my father said in his most soothing tone.

"I didn't know Loretta could climb trees!" I said, giddy over our success.

"Hmmpphh…" Mom replied. "Your sister used to spend more time in trees when she was a kid than she did on the ground. It's a wonder she never fell and broke her neck."

"Loretta used to climb trees when she was little?" I asked, turning to stare at my big sister.

"Actually," Dad said, "I think she used to spend more time up-side-down than she did climbing."

"Up-side-down?"

"Hanging with her legs hooked over a branch," my mother said.

"What are you staring at?" Loretta asked, sounding slightly embarrassed. "We got our Christmas tree, didn't we?"

As we soon discovered, however, what had seemed just about the right size when it was on top of the tree turned out to be rather large after Dad had brought it into the living room.

"I don't know why, but they always look smaller when they're outside," Dad said. "I can cut the bottom row of branches off to make it shorter but I can't make it narrower."

"Couldn't you have found something a *little* smaller?" Mom asked, as she looked at the evergreen branches which extended across the room and nearly touched the davenport.

91

The house had started out as a Norwegian log cabin built by my great-grandfather in the 1800s. The living room had been added to the original four-room house after I was born. The davenport, Mom's easy chair, a rocking chair, the sewing machine, my piano, the buffet, and the television set in the far corner occupied all but a narrow space in the middle of the room.

Dad shook his head. "No, they couldn't have gotten anything smaller. They're all going to be like that. They don't stop growing wider just because they reach a certain height."

After my father cut off the bottom branches, the tree took up a little less room—but not much.

"I guess you won't have to worry about where you're going to put all of the presents this year," Dad said. "You could pack enough for an army under this tree, I think."

Later that afternoon when we had finished decorating our Christmas tree, it looked like we had used only half of the ornaments and lights and tinsel that we usually used.

"I didn't realize there would be this much space to cover," Loretta said.

She paused and reached up to extract a pine needle from her hair. "How did that get there?"

Then she turned her attention toward Mom. "Do you still have the Christmas cards you got last year?" she asked.

My mother nodded. "Yes, they're right here."

Every year, Mom put all of the Christmas cards that came in the mail into a holder that had slots along the edge of it. When the slots were filled with cards, the cards made the shape of a Christmas tree. After Christmas was over, Mom would store the holder and all of the cards in the big box where we kept the rest of the Christmas decorations. The next year, she would read through the cards she had gotten the previous year before she put the new cards into the holder. One time I had asked her why she read the old cards again and she had shrugged and said, "Just because."

"Hmmm," Loretta said. "What if we cut the pictures out of the cards and use some yarn to hang them on the tree?"

"I don't see any reason why we can't," Mom replied. "Actually, it would be a good way to put those old cards to use instead of letting them go to waste."

And so we did. The Christmas card pictures added just the right touch and kept the decorations from looking too skimpy.

Several weeks later on Christmas Eve, as always, our family gathered in the living room to open gifts.

"Is it my imagination," Mom said, "or is the Christmas tree leaning a little bit."

Dad looked at the tree. "It's leaning a little bit, but—"

Before my father could finish his sentence, the tree slowly started to topple over. He leaped to his feet and grabbed the trunk near the top.

"I was afraid it was going to do that eventually," he said. "It's too heavy for the stand."

Ingman helped Dad hold the tree upright while Loretta and I pulled the presents out and crawled underneath to adjust the screws. The tree stand resembled a giant funnel turned upside-down with winter scenes painted on it. I had always thought it would be fun to ride in a one-horse sleigh like the one painted on the tree stand.

"There," Dad said when we were finished adjusting the screws. "I think it will be okay. For now, at least."

All the while that we opened gifts, Mom kept asking the rest of us if we thought the tree was leaning again. Because it was so wide, it was hard to tell if the tree was really leaning, but at least it didn't fall over.

After that, until New Year's Day, walking across the living room was an adventure. Seeing as the Christmas tree had started to fall over once, Dad said we should be careful not to brush against it because there was a good chance that it would do it again. Every time Mom made her way into the living room, she would eye the tree warily, as if it were a bull that might suddenly decide to charge. After I crossed the room to reach my piano or to sit in the rocking chair, I always watched to see if the tree would remain upright. Once, when our dog Needles stood too close and his wagging tail brushed against the lower branches, the tree swayed for a few seconds but then it stopped.

All too soon, New Year's Day arrived, and it was time to take down the tree. Every year, Mom insisted that the tree be taken down on New

Year's Day because once New Year's Day arrived, as far as she was concerned, Christmas was over. All the other times, we had simply re-moved the ornaments and the colored lights and packed them away in the big box we kept in the closet upstairs. But this year, one person had to hold the tree steady while the other person took off the decorations. It was my job to hold the tree.

After what seemed like hours, we were finished.

"Well, this is it until next year," Loretta said, as she closed the box in which we stored our Christmas decorations.

"I'm just glad the tree didn't fall over," Mom said.

Dad lifted the tree out of the stand so he could take it outside. "Even at that, it turned out to be a good Christmas, didn't it," he said.

I couldn't have agreed with him more.

And here I was worried that without a tree, we wouldn't be able to have Christmas. Then my big sister came to our rescue and climbed one of the great big trees to cut off the top. When I didn't even know she could climb trees. Or that she knew how to use a saw.

I guess Loretta wasn't kidding when she said our Christmas tree was going to be surprise.

****

~ 15 ~
A Miracle, Of Sorts

At the front of the church, a twelve-foot spruce tree decorated with ornaments and colored lights stood next to the piano, sheltering a mound of brightly-wrapped gifts. Every year at Christmas, the tree stood in the same spot between the ornately-carved pulpit and the piano.

On the very top of the tree, a glass angel gazed down at the congregation. I was secretly quite proud of the angel because Mom had told me it used to be ours. "But we don't have the right kind of trees on the farm," she'd said. "It doesn't fit too well on long-needled pines, and for the church, the Ladies Aid always insists on spruce trees."

It was a Sunday evening, and a short while ago, we had finished our last Christmas song for the Sunday school program. All of the kids, me included, managed to remember most of the words to the songs and the Bible verses that we had rehearsed over and over. Even though we had made a couple of mistakes during the program, at least no one had fainted or tripped on the steps leading up to the altar.

And now came the really good part.

The presents.

Ever since I'd had to sing *I am So Glad Each Christmas Eve* in Norwegian one year, I was especially relieved when the program was finished because it meant I had once again escaped from singing a solo and could now enjoy the rest of the evening.

In the bright overhead lights, the rectangular panes of the stained-glass windows glowed green, red, amber and blue. I leaned forward and watched intently as two women moved around the church, handing out gifts to the Sunday school children. Just before we went home, we would receive the final gift: a big bright red shiny apple from a large box that was waiting downstairs. I already knew that I was going to share my apple with Dad when I arrived home. My father liked apples as much as I did. When we were ready to eat it, he would take out his pocket knife and cut it into slices—half for me and half for him.

"Mom," I whispered after the women had gone back to the Christmas tree several times, "when am I going to get *my* present."

My mother glanced at me. She was wearing the turquoise wool dress that Loretta had made for her. A gold brooch that was shaped like a stretched out 'S' with a pearl in the middle of it was pinned to the front of her dress.

"Be patient," she murmured. "Patience is a virtue, you know."

I sighed and flopped back against the pew with my arms crossed. Asking me to be patient was about like asking me to sprout wings and fly to the moon. I bounced my legs against the pew in front of me, hoping it would help pass the time.

"Be still," Mom whispered, frowning.

Finally one of the women approached. She looked down at a tag tucked underneath the ribbon. Then she looked at me.

"Here you go," she said.

The package she handed to me was wrapped in pink foil with snow-flake designs on it and was topped by a dark pink ribbon tied in an elegant bow.

"Isn't that a pretty present," Mom remarked.

I was too busy admiring the package to answer her. It was the first gift I had ever received that was tied with a 'real' ribbon, one that went all the way around the box and ended in a bow at the top. The ribbon was an especially pretty color, too, and reminded me of the zinnias Loretta had planted last summer. Not the rusty-orange ones but zinnias that were a vivid, blazing pink. My sister said the color was called fuchsia, and I thought maybe someday I wouldn't mind having a dress that color.

All around me other kids were tearing the paper off their presents. Cries of delight were mingled with the sound of crumpled paper hitting the varnished maple floorboards.

Okay. That was long enough for admiring the outside. Time to see what's inside. But just as I was about to tear off the paper, Mom put her hand on my arm.

"Don't!" she cried out.

I looked up at her, startled. My hand was only inches from the package.

"Let me see that."

Bewildered, I handed her the box.

"Look!" Mom exclaimed.

"What?"

"There's no tape—it's been wrapped without any tape!"

What did she mean, no tape? Christmas presents always needed tape, didn't they?

"See?" Mom said, turning the box toward me.

I bent forward. She was right. The box didn't have any tape. The ends of the paper were folded neatly against each other, and there wasn't one single piece of tape.

"How'd they do that?"

"I don't know," Mom admitted. "Must have taken a long time, though."

As we both gazed at the box, suddenly I didn't feel like just ripping the paper.

"Aren't you going to open it?" Mom inquired after a bit.

"How?" I asked.

"Untie the ribbon. Then take one of the ends very carefully and pull it out."

I did as she suggested, and when I unfolded a flap on one end, the paper fell away from the box in a single, perfect piece.

"It's such pretty paper. Do you think we should save it?" Mom asked.

"Could we?"

My mother nodded and carefully folded the pink foil and the ribbon and then tucked it all into her purse while I went about discovering what was inside the box—a book of Bible stories that was just for kids. If it had been up to me, I would have chosen a book about horses, but of course, just as long as it was a book, I liked it.

From the time I had been a very little girl and had picked out Little Golden books while Mom shopped for groceries at the store in town, I had enjoyed getting books.

As I leafed through my latest acquisition, my mother took the box and hunted among the folds of white tissue paper until she found a small card. We always drew names in Sunday school, and she wanted to find out who had given me the gift so I could thank the proper person.

A short while later, after all the thank-yous had been exchanged and the crumpled pieces of wrapping paper had been picked up and put into a big cardboard box, we went downstairs for lunch.

Next to the presents, lunch was my second-favorite part of the Christmas program. Even as I munched my way through Christmas cookies, lefse, sandbakelse, buttered nut bread, and homemade dill pickles, I could hardly wait until it was time to go home. I wanted to tell Dad about the Christmas present that didn't have any tape. I was pretty sure he wouldn't believe me. Good thing Mom had tucked the paper into her purse.

Loretta had driven us to church. She had been busy with her own Sunday school class and had not seen the gift before I opened it. When I told her about the present that had been wrapped without a single piece of tape, she agreed it must have been a difficult task. Loretta was good at wrapping presents, but she said she wouldn't want to try it without using any tape.

By the time we were settled into the car, I knew exactly how I would tell Dad about my present. The apple I had chosen from the big box in the church basement was tucked safely inside my coat pocket. Mom said I should put it in my coat pocket so it wouldn't freeze. Although it was not as cold as it would be later on in January, I was still glad we didn't live far from the church and that we would soon be in our nice warm kitchen. Of course, if we lived farther away from the church, the car heater would have time to warm up enough to start putting out heat, but all things considered, I was just as well satisfied that we didn't have to drive very far. The anticipation of telling Dad about the present wrapped without any tape was almost more than I could stand.

When we reached the top of the first hill between the church and our farm, I realized I would have to wait to tell Dad. The lights were still on in the barn, and that meant my father wasn't finished with chores yet.

My mother noticed the barn lights too.

"I thought Dad would be done by now," she said. "I hope he's not having trouble with something."

My sister shrugged. "It's only nine o'clock," she said. "We decided to have the program an hour earlier this year. Remember? So it wouldn't get so late for the kids since they still have school tomorrow."

"Oh, right," Mom said. "I still would have thought he'd be finished by now, though."

"When we get home, want me to go out and see what's taking so long?" I asked.

My mother shook her head. "No, no. That's all right. Change your clothes and put them away. I'm sure he'll be in by the time you have your pajamas on."

Half an hour later, after I had set my apple on the table where Dad would see it and then had put on my pajamas, had hung up my red wool skirt and the white blouse, and had rolled up my white leotards and put them in my drawer, Dad finally came in the house.

That half-hour wait had seemed like an eternity.

Under other circumstances, I would have been curious about what had taken so long. Anything from a plugged vacuum line to a newborn calf could delay the chores. Tonight I didn't even think to ask, and while my father untied his work shoes, I retrieved the pink foil from Mom's purse.

"Did you have fun at the Christmas program?" Dad asked, removing his shoes and setting them in their customary spot near the door.

I held out the pink foil. "Look what my present was wrapped in."

Dad squinted at the paper and nodded. "Pretty paper."

"No, Daddy!"

He glanced at me quizzically. "It's NOT pretty paper?"

"Yes, Dad, it is. But—that's not it. Look."

He squinted at the piece of foil once again and then shook his head.

"I don't see anything."

I heaved a deep sigh, thinking I probably should have known Dad wouldn't be able to spot the obvious, although, to tell you the truth, I had noticed that my father and my big brother didn't seem very interested in certain things. Such as the way presents were wrapped. Or which clothes they were going to wear for a special event. Or whether their hair looked the way it was supposed to.

I held out the paper. "See? Right here, where it came together around the box. It didn't have any tape."

"I've never seen anything like it," Mom added. "It must have taken a long, long time to do it that way."

Dad shook his head. "No, it doesn't take long. Not really."

My mother frowned.

So did I.

"And how," she retorted, "would you know?"

I wondered the same thing myself.

"Because," Dad said, "when we lived in Waukesha, I used to watch Grandma do it this way. It's not that hard. All you have to do is measure the box and measure the paper so it comes out even."

When Dad was a little boy, he had lived with his grandmother for a while. Grandma Zinderman, I had been told, was particular about cleaning her house. Each day had been devoted to a special cleaning task, and once a week, she had gotten down on her hands and knees to scrub the floor with a scrub brush and a bar of lye soap. She also had owned a German shepherd named Happy who had once arrived home carrying a package of meat wrapped in white butcher paper. They never did figure out where Happy had acquired the meat.

"Wait a minute," I said. "You mean you already *knew* about presents wrapped without any tape?"

"Sure," Dad replied looking back and forth between Mom and me, "didn't you?"

I considered asking him why he would think we already knew. Every Christmas that I could remember, Dad had reached for his pocket knife (which was the same pocket knife he used to cut apples) so he could slice through layers of tape and wrapping paper, muttering that he didn't know why my mother always used enough of each to choke a horse.

And he was right.

Sometimes one of the women's magazines my sister subscribed to published articles about how to wrap gifts, especially oddly-shaped packages. My mother always read the articles carefully. And not just once but two or three times. Then she would get out the wrapping paper and tape and would start wrapping presents, mumbling the instructions under her breath. In the end, the packages still looked as if they had been wrapped by a gorilla or a blind one-armed monkey (her words, not mine). Mom always said that she was glad tape didn't cost very much because otherwise, she would end up bankrupt at Christmas time.

Once or twice, my mother had even tried telling me how to wrap the gifts, her theory being that if she gave enough detailed instructions, and that if she repeated them often enough, then perhaps the presents would end up looking better.

I didn't have any more success than she did.

No wonder Mom and I thought the gift wrapped without any tape seemed like such a miracle.

****

~ 16 ~
Ivory Snow

Loretta stood by the kitchen cupboard. In front of her was the large mixing bowl she used for baking cookies. Beside it were two boxes of Ivory soap flakes.

"What'cha doin'?" I asked.

It was a Sunday afternoon, and in just a little while, we were going to start decorating the Christmas tree.

My sister opened a drawer and pulled out the spoon she used to make cookie dough. "What am I doing?" she said. "I'm mixing soap flakes."

She picked up a box and dumped some into the bowl.

I could see that she was mixing soap flakes.

What I didn't know was why.

"What are you going to mix them with?" I asked, hoping she wouldn't say cookie dough. I couldn't imagine why she would mix soap flakes with cookie dough, but since she had gotten out the cookie bowl and the cookie spoon, the idea didn't seem all that far-fetched.

"Don't worry. I'm not putting soap flakes into cookies," my sister replied. "I'm going to mix the soap flakes with water."

As Loretta reached into the cupboard for a measuring cup, I wondered how she knew that I had been thinking about cookie dough.

"Why are you mixing soap flakes with water?" I asked.

Loretta moved to the sink and turned on the tap.

"So we can decorate the Christmas tree," she replied.

After sitting in the barn for a week, our Christmas tree was now completely thawed, and earlier this afternoon, Dad had brought it into the living room and set it up. Most years when we cut our Christmas tree, the temperature outside was below freezing, and the tree often was covered with snow.

One time I had asked Dad why the Christmas tree couldn't thaw in the house. Even though the heat that the cows gave off kept the barn from freezing, the barn wasn't nearly as warm as the house, so it seemed to take an awfully long time for our Christmas tree to thaw. Dad had pointed out that my mother would not appreciate puddles of water on the living room floor.

After he mentioned it, I could see how it would be better to have puddles of water on the barn floor rather than in the living room.

When Dad was satisfied that the tree was anchored firmly in the tree stand, he had brought the big box of Christmas decorations downstairs so my mother could begin unpacking the strings of lights, the tinsel, and the colored glass balls. Every year we decorated the tree with lights and tinsel and ornaments. As far as I could recall, we had never used soap on the tree. Everything else that spent time in the barn (coats, boots, hats, mittens, gloves) ended up smelling like cow manure, but for some reason, the Christmas tree came out of the barn smelling like a Christmas tree. Still, my sister seemed to spend much of her time on weekends cleaning, so maybe she had decided the tree wasn't clean enough to be in the house after sitting in the barn for a week.

"You're mixing up soap flakes so we can wash the Christmas tree before we decorate it?" I asked.

"No, silly, we're not going to wash the tree," Loretta said." We're going to flock it."

"Flock? What's that mean?"

Loretta picked up the spoon and began mixing the soap flakes.

"Flock means to make it look like snow," she explained.

Loretta stopped mixing and added more water. She stirred for a while, then she added more soap flakes. A few minutes later, she opened the drawer and took out a heavy-duty wire whisk. The whisk had been inside a bag of powdered milk replacer my father had bought for the calves. Dad said he didn't need the whisk in the barn, that the wooden paddle he used for mixing milk replacer worked just fine, but that maybe Mom and Loretta could use it in the house. The whisk, as it turned out, came in handy for mixing pancake batter.

"Why are you using that?" I asked.

"To make it fluffy," Loretta replied, "so it'll look like snow."

I peered into the bowl as my sister went to work with the whisk.

Didn't look much like snow to me. It looked more like a sloppy mess.

"After we put the lights and ornaments on, we're going to put this on the branches," Loretta explained. "Then the tree will look like it's covered with snow."

I watched in silence as she continued mixing.

Now that I had thought about it for a bit, I could see how the stuff in the bowl MIGHT look like snow once it was on the Christmas tree.

"Where'd you find out about using soap flakes to make snow?" I asked after a while.

"Magazine," Loretta replied. "There, that should do it."

She tapped the whisk on the side of the bowl. A glob of soap hung there for a second before sliding off.

"The article said to mix it up first so it has time to thicken before you put it on the tree," Loretta explained.

She picked up the bowl and the spoon and went into the living room—with me right on her heels. Ever since I was big enough to walk, I had known that if I didn't stick close to my big sister, I might miss something important.

As was the case every year, we started by putting on the egg-shaped lights: red and green and white and blue and yellow. When Loretta looped the string of lights in one hand so she could start hanging them on the tree, the bulbs clacked together with a hollow sound. She began on the bottom, clipping each light to a small branch, and then she worked her way around the front and then to the back by the picture window. I reached behind the tree as far as I could until I felt the string in my hand, then I pulled it through to my side. Loretta came back to where I was standing and started the whole process again, winding the lights around and around, until the last light was at the top where it would illuminate the star we would place on the uppermost branch.

Mom said the lights we had now were a big improvement over the old ones we used to have. When a bulb burned out on the old-fashioned strings of lights, it had taken a long time to remove each bulb and then put in another one to find the culprit, because if one bulb burned out, the whole string wouldn't light. But on the new ones, she said, only the bulb that was burned out wouldn't light, so you could see right away which one was causing the problem.

I was glad we didn't have the old-fashioned lights anymore. Otherwise putting lights on the tree would have taken longer yet.

After we had arranged the lights to my sister's satisfaction, making sure that they weren't too close together or that they weren't too far apart, we began to hang the red, blue, silver, gold and green glass ball ornaments.

The blue ornaments were my favorite because they were the color of the blue herons that came to nest by the creek at the bottom of the pasture during the summer. The first year that the pair of herons had appeared, Dad said he thought they were only stopping for a rest and to find frogs to eat. But the herons had stayed the whole summer and had returned the next year. I had never seen a blue heron before, and it was fun to watch the birds as they waded around in the marsh. We could see them from the front yard, although even when I walked down to the mailbox to get the mail for Mom, they didn't seem to mind that anyone was so close to them. The blue glass ornaments reminded me that maybe next summer I would once again have a chance to watch the herons.

When the last ornament had been placed on the tree, one more step remained.

"What about the tinsel?" I asked.

To my way of thinking, a Christmas tree was not a Christmas tree without 'icicles.' That's what Dad called tinsel—icicles. The tinsel was made out of thin strands of aluminum foil, and after we took it off the tree, we laid it across a big piece of newspaper and folded the paper over so the tinsel wouldn't become bent and crinkly after it was packed away in the big box with the lights and ornaments.

Loretta shook her head. "We're not going to put tinsel on the tree this year. I think the flocking will be enough."

Ah, yes, the soap.

"How are you supposed to get that stuff on the branches?" I asked.

My big sister reached for the bowl. "The article said to just dab it on with the spoon.

A few seconds later, the first lump of 'snow' was on the tree.

"Oh, this is going to be pretty," Loretta said.

"I think so, too," said Mom, who had been watching us decorate. One result of the polio that had afflicted my mother sixteen years before I was born was that she couldn't stand up long enough with nothing to lean on to put ornaments on a Christmas tree.

By the time my sister had used the whole bowl, the tree wasn't just pretty, it was downright beautiful.

And the tree stayed beautiful, too...up until Mom decided she felt cold about five minutes later. The sun had started to set, taking with it the warm sunshine that had come in through the big picture window for most of the afternoon. My mother frequently complained of feeling cold. She said it was because she couldn't move around very much.

Mom turned to me. "Would you please go out to the porch and get some more wood?"

About six feet away from the Christmas tree stood a wood stove. During the winter, it was my job to fill the woodbox that sat in the porch if Dad didn't have time to fill it. Whether my father had time to fill the woodbox often depended upon whether the tractor started that day or if the barn cleaner or the manure spreader had frozen up.

I didn't really mind filling the woodbox, although I had noticed that Dad could do the job much faster. He could carry twice as many pieces of wood on each trip from the pile by the shed to the woodbox in the porch.

I went out to the porch and retrieved an armful of firewood. When I returned to the living room, I saw the full effect of the Christmas tree. In the gathering darkness, the colored lights lit up the snow that my sister had dabbed onto the dark green branches. Each clump of snow was a different color, and I wondered if lights on a tree outside that had real snow would look the same.

I put the wood into a cardboard box we kept in the living room. Then my mother loaded the woodstove. Red-hot coals remained in the bottom from the last time she had put wood in the stove not long after dinner. In short order, the wood had ignited and a little while later, the room was starting to warm up nicely.

So was the Christmas tree.

As the spicy scent of warm pine needles grew stronger, one by one, the clumps of snow began to slide off the branches.

Well—not all of the snow fell off. Just on the side nearest the stove.

"Oh, *no!*" Loretta wailed.

I started to giggle, but Mom shot such a fierce look in my direction that I clammed up.

Loretta tried mixing more soap flakes, but the flocking still refused to stick.

Dad thought the tree looked realistic.

"Snow falls off outside, too, when it warms up on a sunny day," he said.

His observation made my sister feel only slightly better.

"I should have known," she said, as she surveyed the lopsided Christmas tree. "It sounded much too easy."

And that was both the first and the last time we had a flocked Christmas tree—which was unfortunate, because the 'snow' really was quite lovely.

Or at least the snow that stayed on the tree was lovely.

****

~ 17 ~
A Candle For Christmas

The elementary school cafeteria was strangely quiet. During the morning when we came here for our milk break, we could hear the cooks in the kitchen making dinner. The clatter of pans and covers and people talking and moving back and forth between the sinks and stoves meant that in only a few hours, lunch would be ready. But now at this time of the afternoon, the deserted kitchen was silent. Even the lights had been turned off, although I could still smell the pine cleaner the cooks had used to wash the floor.

All of the Brownies, me included, were clustered around one of the long tables where we ate lunch. School was over for the day, and while the other students had gotten on their buses, or if they lived in town, had already started to walk home, those of us who were in Brownies had stayed for our weekly meeting.

Last week, just before the meeting was finished, the Brownie leaders had told us that this week we were going to make candles that could be used as centerpieces to give to our mothers for Christmas.

I had never seen any candles around our house, or any centerpieces, for that matter, and I wondered what Mom would think about getting a candle for Christmas.

"The first thing we're going to do today is decide what color you want to make your candles," said one of the Brownie leaders. We had two leaders, one with dark-brown hair and the other with sandy-red hair.

"Is that what the crayons are for?" asked one girl.

Both Brownie leaders nodded. "You need to find four or five of the same color," said one.

Two plastic ice cream buckets half filled with well-used crayons stood on the table in front of us.

"Where did you find so many?" asked another girl.

The Brownie leader with dark hair laughed. "Some of these are from my own kids," she said. "The rest are from my neighbor. She could hardly believe her ears when I said I wanted crayons. Her kids are all grown up, and she was glad to get rid of them."

"Lucky for us," said one girl.

The Brownie leader smiled. "Yes, very lucky for us."

"Let's not waste time," said the other leader. "If we're going to finish today, you have to pick a color right now."

A few seconds later, we were busily hunting through the crayons that one of the leaders had dumped out on the table, and it was almost like putting a puzzle together.

"I've got a dark blue," someone said. "Is there another pink?"

"Here," I said, handing over a pink crayon.

"Did anybody find a purple?" asked another girl.

"Violet-blue all right?" someone else replied.

"What about red?" asked another. "Did anybody find more red?"

All the other girls knew what colors they wanted, but I still hadn't decided. If it were strictly up to me, I would have picked blue or purple. But this wasn't supposed to be my candle. It was going to be Mom's. Now what color would she like?

And then I remembered.

My mother's favorite color was yellow. She said she liked yellow because it was the color of sunshine. With my blond hair, yellow made me look as though I had rubbed dandelions all over my face. But Mom's hair was dark, and she looked pretty in yellow.

"Did anybody find a yellow?" I asked.

Surprisingly enough, only one true yellow was hidden in the bunch. You would think, among all of those crayons, that there would have to be more than one yellow. But there wasn't.

"What do you suppose happened to all of the yellow?" asked the leader with the sandy-red hair.

The other leader shrugged. "My neighbor apologized and said there wouldn't be much yellow because her daughters liked to draw pictures of dandelions when they were little. She said she never could figure out why they were so crazy about dandelions, but they used to have contests to see who could color the biggest flowers."

"Well, one won't be enough," said the first leader. She paused and tapped her finger against her lips.

"What if we mix some colors?" she continued. "Here's an orange-yellow...and two yellow-oranges...and maybe you could use this orange one, too."

The orange-yellow and the two yellow-oranges were about twice as long as the only true yellow, and with the piece of orange added in, there would be just enough to make a candle, the Brownie leader said.

The project involved melting the crayons with paraffin wax in a double boiler and then pouring the hot mixture over ice cubes that had been placed in milk cartons. The ice cubes would hold the wick until the wax hardened, the leaders said, and after the ice melted, the candles would have interesting patterns.

Our milk at home came from the cows in our barn and was stored in the refrigerator in a white ceramic pitcher my mother said had belonged to her mother. I had never touched a milk carton before. When I picked one up, I noticed that it felt smooth and waxy, like the boxes our butter came in. About once a week, Mom would order butter from the milk hauler, and then he would leave it in the milkhouse.

The Brownie leaders used two hot plates to heat the paraffin and crayons, but even at that, it took a long time to make a dozen candles, one for each of us. While the paraffin and crayons melted, we were kept busy getting trays of ice cubes from the freezer in the kitchen so we could fill two more milk cartons. The top of the cartons had been pulled apart to open them up, and it took many ice cubes to fill each one.

"My mom likes candles, but she's never had a candle this big," said one girl.

Finally the last batch of paraffin had been poured into the last container.

"We're going to let these sit until next week," one of leaders explained. "Then we'll tear off the milk carton and there will be your candle."

At the next meeting the following week, we could hardly wait to see what our candles looked like. Tearing off the milk cartons was a little like peeling an orange. A couple of the girls said they knew their mothers would put the candles in the middle of the table during Thanksgiving dinner and Christmas dinner because their mothers always burned candles at Thanksgiving and Christmas.

Seeing as we'd never had any candles around our house, I wondered if Mom would burn her candle.

One by one—as the piles of torn milk cartons grew—the candles emerged until they stood in a row on the cafeteria table. Just like the leaders said, they were filled with interesting holes where the ice had melted. Blue ones and red ones and green ones and purple ones and pink ones.

And one very odd-looking orange-yellow candle.

As I looked at the row of candles, a lump rose in my throat, and my chest started to feel tight, the way it did when I knew I was going to cry. Not only was my candle the ugliest color of all, but it also wasn't the kind of yellow Mom liked. It was much more orange than yellow, and it reminded me of mustard mixed with ketchup.

While the leaders explained that we had to let the candles sit for another week so the water could dry out of the crevices, I stood there blinking back tears. I did not want to cry because if I started crying, then everyone would want to know what was wrong. And I would rather not call more attention to my candle than was absolutely necessary.

At our next meeting, only the week before Christmas, we wrapped the candles in white paper that we had decorated ourselves. Decorating the paper had involved using potatoes that were cut in half. The leaders had carved Christmas tree designs in the potatoes, and then we had dipped them in green finger paint and had stamped them all over the paper. The Brownie leaders said that instead of worrying about folding corners, we would wrap the candles the way that bottles are wrapped, with the paper gathered at the top and tied with a ribbon.

When my candle was finally wrapped, I felt a little better. At least now I didn't have to see it sitting next to all of the other much prettier candles.

A short while later, it was time to go home. Dad had driven into town to pick me up, as he always did, and I was relieved to see that Mom had not accompanied him. Sometimes my mother rode into town with Dad and sometimes she didn't. It all depended upon what we were having for supper and whether she could spare any time away from the kitchen. The inside of the car was filled with familiar odor of cow manure and barn lime that always clung to my father's chore clothes. When he was only driving into town to pick me up, Dad didn't bother to change his clothes first.

"What's in the package," he asked as I closed the car door and settled back into the seat.

"Mom's Christmas present," I said.

"What is it?"

I hesitated before answering. "Do you promise not to tell?"

Dad nodded. "Wouldn't be a surprise if I told her what it was."

"It's a candle," I said.

"A candle?" Dad said. "You made a candle? I'll bet Ma is going to like that. What color is it?"

"Well," I said, "it's...umm...it's yellow. Kind of."

When we arrived home, I discovered that Mom had gone downstairs to get potatoes for supper. Usually it was my job to fetch potatoes, but since I hadn't been home, Mom had made the trip herself. I knew that my mother would still be downstairs for a little while yet, because it always took her an awfully long time to go up and down the basement steps, so I quickly carried the candle upstairs to the bedroom I shared with Loretta and hid it in my dresser drawer.

Although I wasn't sure whether I wanted to give the candle to Mom after all, a week later on Christmas Eve, I retrieved the package from upstairs and handed it to her.

"What is this?" she asked.

"We made it at Brownies," I said.

My mother slipped the ribbon off the top, pulled open the paper and reached inside.

"Why," she said, turning the candle around and around, "it's a candle. I've never gotten a candle for Christmas...and it's such a. . .well. . . it's such an. . . .an. . . interesting color...very unusual..."

"Are you going to burn it?" I asked.

"Certainly not," she replied. "Because if I burn it, then it will melt and be ruined, and I don't want it to be ruined."

Now that I had gotten another good look at the candle, I was re-minded all over again of why I thought it was an ugly color. Personally, I couldn't see what difference it would make if it got ruined.

"What are you going to do with your candle, Ma?" Dad asked.

"It's a Christmas present," my mother replied, "so...it's going to be my Christmas candle. I've never had a candle for Christmas."

For several years, my mother kept the candle with the Christmas decorations, and each year, she would unwrap it and would set it out on a frilly white doily she had crocheted. And each year when Mom put the candle back in the box, I was glad that I didn't have to look at it anymore. Why—oh, why—did my mother's candle have to turn out to be that particular color?

Then one year, a couple of mice found their way inside our farmhouse and nested inside the Christmas box. The mice must have really liked wax. When we were ready to decorate the Christmas tree and my sister had brought the ornaments downstairs, my mother sat before the open box, speechless. I peered over her shoulder and saw gnawed pieces of orange-yellow wax scattered over everything.

The candle itself was nothing but a stump.

"Oh, NO!" Mom cried. "Look what those mice did to my candle! They destroyed it! And it was so pretty, too."

"Pretty?" I said, wondering if maybe my ears were playing tricks on me.

She nodded. "Very pretty. Like the color of the sun just before it starts to set sometimes. You know—when it's going to be a sailor's sun."

"A sailor's sun?"

"'Red at night, sailor's delight,'" she said. "It's an old saying that means we're going to have a nice day tomorrow."

All this time, my mother thought the candle was pretty because it reminded her of the sun when it's starting to set?

And here I thought it resembled mustard-mixed-with-ketchup.

But you know what? I liked Mom's idea better. Much better.

Except that now it was too late. The mice had already chewed the candle to bits...

****

Directions for making candles out of crayons and paraffin wax are included in Appendix B.

~ 18 ~
It's The Thought That Counts

M y mother was sitting by the table when I opened the kitchen door. "Would you help me wrap a Christmas present this afternoon?" she asked.

"Me?" I said.

I had only just arrived home from school and hadn't even changed out of my school clothes yet. Every day when I got home from school, I put on old clothes so I wouldn't ruin my school clothes when I went out to the barn. Anything can happen when you're out in the barn. You could catch your pants on a nail that's sticking out from the front of the calf manger, for one thing, which is why a certain pair of pants that I wore for chores now had a patch just above the knee.

Every day when I came home from school, I also ate a snack. It was a long time between lunch at school and supper at home, so a piece of cake or a couple of cookies helped quiet the rumbling in my stomach. One of my favorite snacks was Mom's pineapple-up-side-down-cake with maraschino cherries in the middle of the pineapple rings. I also liked fresh homemade bread covered with butter and blackberry jam. But of course, lefse was my all-time favorite. And with any luck at all, there would still be some left from the last batch Mom had baked.

"Why do you want me to help you wrap a present?" I asked as I moved my school books from the table to the steps so I wouldn't forget to take them upstairs with me later.

"The box is kind of big for me to handle," Mom explained, "and if you help, maybe it won't look like it was wrapped by a blind one-armed monkey."

My mother had always been embarrassed about the way she wrapped gifts, especially larger boxes. Mom's legs were not strong enough to hold her up for very long at a time, so she had to do almost everything sitting down, and it seemed as if the wrapping paper and the tape never wanted to cooperate. When Loretta wrapped presents, she either spread everything out on the floor in front of her, or else she used the sewing table

Dad had built. I had never seen my big sister sit down in a chair to wrap Christmas presents.

"Couldn't you ask Loretta to wrap it?" I asked.

Loretta was an expert at wrapping gifts. Each of the packages she wrapped ended up with neatly folded corners and a straight, perfect seam along the bottom.

Mom shook her head. "I'd rather get it wrapped right now, if I could, before your father comes in for supper. Besides, I can't ask Loretta to do everything for me. I don't like to feel completely helpless, you know."

I really wasn't sure how much help I would be. I wasn't much good at wrapping presents myself, even though I had watched Loretta do it many times. But, if Mom wanted me to help her, I would try.

A little while later, my mother was seated by the kitchen table with a roll of wrapping paper, the tape and the scissors. The paper she had chosen was decorated with red and pink poinsettias that had green leaves edged with gold and silver. Of all the wrapping paper we had this year, it was my favorite.

"Now all I need is the box," Mom said. "Would you please go into the closet—"

She stopped and shook her head. "No, never mind. I guess I'd better do it myself. You're not supposed to look in the closets, and there are a couple of things I don't want you to see."

My mother reached for her crutches and then made her way to the closet in the small hallway between the kitchen and the bathroom.

Although I couldn't see what she was doing, I could hear various thumps and bumps, and I was almost beside myself with curiosity.

Then I heard the closet door slide shut.

"Okay, would you please put this on the table?" Mom asked.

'This' turned out to be a rather large ordinary cardboard box with the flaps folded underneath each other.

"What is it?" I asked.

"It's one of those blanket-lined denim chore coats your father likes. His old one is so worn out that I told him he should buy a new one. He said they were too expensive and that he could still wear his old one for a while yet."

"Did you get it today?" I wondered.

When my mother wanted to go Christmas shopping, Dad, Loretta or Ingman drove her to town. Loretta was at work now, though. So was Ingman. And that left just Dad. But under the circumstances, I knew Mom wouldn't ask Dad to take her shopping.

"No, I didn't get it today. I told your sister just exactly what I wanted, and she bought one for me last weekend. I hope he likes it," Mom said.

I was sure that my father would like the chore coat. His old one was in bad shape. For one thing, the zipper tab was gone, and the only way he could zip it up was by using his pliers. Dad always kept a pliers in the little pocket on the leg of his overalls. Sometimes it took him a few minutes to zip his coat. Once the zipper was lined up, there was a trick to positioning the pliers just right so he could grasp the tiny piece of metal where the zipper tab used to be and then pull the zipper all the way closed without letting go of it.

Dad also didn't dare put anything in the coat pockets, such as his chore gloves, because they would quickly work their way out of the large holes in the bottom. My father was especially reluctant to put his chore gloves into his pocket, I had noticed, after one had fallen into a pile of cow manure. Mom had tried to mend the pockets a couple of times, but by now, there wasn't much left to mend.

On the other hand, I wasn't surprised that Dad figured he could still wear his old coat for a while yet. My parents both firmly believed in getting their money's worth out of things. Mom said it was because they had lived through the Great Depression. During the Depression, a new shirt only cost twenty-five cents, she said, except that no one had twenty-five cents.

My mother sat down by the table and pulled the box toward her. "Now let's see if we can get this wrapped," she said. "I suppose I should tape the box shut first."

Mom disentangled the flaps that had been folded together against themselves and smoothed them out as best she could. As I tore off pieces of tape and handed them to her, she put them on the box flaps, six on each side. Then she put more tape along the middle where the flaps came together.

"That ought to do it," she said.

"How come you have to tape the flaps down like that?" I asked.

"I don't want them to pop open after we put the paper on it."

"What would happen if the flaps popped open?"

"The present would have a bulge on top. And the strain might cause the rest of the tape on the wrapping paper to let go. Once I wrap a present, I want to be sure it stays wrapped until it's ready to be opened."

The next step required cutting a piece of wrapping paper that was large enough to go around the box. When my mother was halfway down the length of the roll, she stopped and handed the scissors to me.

"You're going to have to finish. I can't reach that far. Not sitting down. If I could stand up, then I could do it myself," she said.

I took the scissors and finished cutting along the roll.

Then it was my job to turn the box this way and that as my mother taped the wrapping paper into place.

"You'll have to cut another piece. It won't reach across the bottom," Mom said.

I cut off another strip of wrapping paper, and then we taped it along the bottom to cover the part of the box that still showed.

After we had finished taping the wrapping paper, it was my job to hold the box upright so Mom could get at the ends better.

"I know you're supposed to fold the paper and trim it off, but every time I do that, I cut off too much," she explained.

"What happens if you cut off too much?"

"Then we'd have to take more paper and tape along the ends to cover the box, and we would be working at cross purposes."

"What does 'cross purposes' mean?"

"You do one thing to accomplish something but end up making more work for yourself in the long run," Mom explained.

Instead of trimming the paper, she folded it over and used some tape to hold it in place.

Well, not just 'some' tape. A lot of tape. Many long lengths of tape.

When we were finished, the wrapping paper was bunched up on the ends in big wads. I noticed, too, that we had somehow managed to cut the paper crooked so the pattern was off-kilter. Either that, or we hadn't positioned the box evenly in the center of the paper. The crooked poinsettias made the box look as if it were sitting at an angle, even though I knew that it was not.

My mother sighed as she looked at the lumpy, lopsided package. "No matter how hard I try, I'm simply no good at this," she said.

Although I wasn't going to say anything because I didn't want to hurt my mother's feelings, I had to admit that the present wasn't quite as pretty as the ones Loretta wrapped.

Mom shrugged and shook her head. "Well, what's done is done. At least it's wrapped. Let's put it back in the closet."

I carried the box over to the closet for Mom, and then, as I waited in the kitchen, I once again heard various thumps and bumps while my mother put it away.

"Thank you," Mom said when she came back into the kitchen. "I was starting to worry that Dad might accidentally see his present before I could get it wrapped. He looked in the closet this afternoon for that old cap of his with the ear flaps, and I didn't want to take any more chances."

"Is there some lefse left?" I asked.

My mother threw a startled glance in my direction. "I'm sorry," she said. "You haven't even eaten a snack yet. Yes, there's a couple of pieces. I've been saving them for you."

When Christmas Eve arrived, I could hardly wait for Dad to open the present that Mom and I had wrapped. Ingman was usually elected to pass out the gifts, and when he handed the box to Dad, I stopped opening the gift that my brother had set in front of me a little while ago so I could watch Dad open his present.

My father held up the box, as if he were testing the weight. "Must be, what? Half a pound of tape on here?" he said.

My mother assumed her most dignified expression. "I did the best I could."

Dad grinned and then took out his pocket knife and began to slice through all the layers of tape. It was like watching him open an envelope with his pocket knife, except that it didn't take him this long to open an envelope.

After he had sawed through the tape on both ends, he used the pocket knife to cut the tape along the bottom. Then he put the pocket knife back into his pocket, and several minutes later, he removed the last of the paper.

"Oops," Dad said, "I guess I still need my knife for the box, don't I."

Out came the pocket knife again so Dad could cut the tape Mom had put on the ends and along the top seam. At last, he was able to open the flaps.

"Hey!" he exclaimed, pulling the chore coat out of the box. "This is just what I need. I could really use one of these!"

"Is it the right kind?" Mom asked.

Dad nodded. He stood up, slipped into the coat, zipped it, and then held his arms in front of him at chest level and flexed them back and forth.

"Fits just perfect," he said. "Now I won't have to worry about losing my gloves."

"And you don't have to use your pliers to zip it up," I said.

"Nope. Although for a little while there, I thought I was going to have to use my pliers to pull off all of that tape."

My mother frowned. "When I wrap a present, Roy, I want to make sure that it stays wrapped," she declared.

"Oh," Dad said, "it 'stayed' all right."

Mom's warning glance was enough to convince my father that perhaps he ought to let the subject drop.

Every day for the rest of the winter—long after the wrapping paper and the box had been discarded—Dad wore the coat. And on several occasions, he made a point of telling Mom it was one of the best Christmas presents he had ever gotten.

Okay, so maybe my mother wasn't all that great at wrapping presents. But I think Dad would have been the first to agree that she was good at knowing what to put inside. And isn't that what really counts?

****

~ 19 ~
The Circus Pony

I could scarcely believe my eyes. The thermometer outside the kitchen window said it was twenty degrees below zero.

Again.

Not that I was surprised. It seemed that most years right around Christmas the weather turned cold and the thermometer would drop far below zero overnight.

This was getting out of hand, though.

I flopped down in a chair and heaved a sigh gusty enough to ruffle my bangs. In a few days I would be going back to school after the holiday break, and I despaired of ever being able to use my brand new Christmas present.

Dad glanced up from eating his breakfast. He had come in from doing the morning milking fifteen minutes ago. Before sitting down at the table, he had washed his hands and his face and had slicked back his hair with a wet comb. Although Dad's hair was still dark on top, both sides of his head were silvery gray.

"What's wrong?" he asked.

"It's cold outside!" I wailed.

My father nodded as he lifted a forkful of pancakes toward his mouth.

"Usually is when we get to this time of year. We do live in Wisconsin, you know."

"But Christmas vacation is almost over!"

"Then you'll be going back to school, I guess."

It was obvious that he didn't get the point.

"Daa-aad! When it's cold like this, it's too cold to ride Dusty!"

My father rubbed his ear. "Yup. You'd only be outside a few minutes before your hands and feet got numb."

I regarded him with deepening suspicion. "Did you forget about my Christmas present?"

"Present?" he asked, frowning. "What pres...Oh...THAT."

120

For more than half of my life, I had spent a tremendous amount of time begging, pleading and wishing for a pony, and finally my dream had come true. But ever since the summer before last, I had been riding my dappled brown pony bareback. Then my big brother, Ingman, had gotten me a pony saddle for Christmas this year.

I hadn't minded riding my pony bareback. In fact, I had become quite good at it. Every time Dusty and I went for a ride, however, Mom would make me put on a clean pair of pants when I came back into the house. "Don't sit down on anything. Your pants are filthy," she would say.

During the summer, when it was too hot to wear jeans, then I had to wash my legs and put on a clean pair of shorts every time I rode my pony.

The saddle, it seemed to me, would solve both problems.

I had named the pony Dusty because she was dark brown with light brown dapples which looked as if someone had dusted her with a powder puff. After I had the pony for a while, I realized it was a good name in other ways, too, because Dusty enjoyed rolling in the dirt. Dad said all horses rolled to scratch their backs or to escape the flies or to dry off when they were sweaty. Dusty must have had an exceptionally itchy back or else the flies liked her a lot. She rolled every day during the summer.

As Christmas had drawn closer this year, one day Ingman had asked if I would like a pony saddle. Of course I said, 'yes!' Cowboys rode their horses with saddles, and if there was one thing I had always wanted to be, it was a cowboy. Mom said my big brother worked hard at the creamery to earn his money and that he should buy something for himself, instead. Ingman had grinned, showing off his very white and very even teeth, and said he didn't need anything for himself.

The day before Christmas Eve, we had found the saddle at a store called Fleet Farm in the city where my sister worked. It was the most beautiful little saddle I had ever seen. The seat was black and the rest was brown tooled leather. It even had a shiny silver saddle horn.

I knew Dusty was going to look extremely smart wearing her brand new saddle. Or at least I thought she would if the weather ever warmed up enough so I could try it out. Even though we had gotten the saddle only a week ago, it seemed more like a month. On Christmas Eve the weather had turned bitterly cold. And it had been cold ever since.

As I sat at the breakfast table with Dad, once again I heaved a sigh gusty enough to ruffle my bangs.

My father smiled. "Tell you what. Why don't you ride Dusty this afternoon. I'll help you put the saddle on."

What was Dad talking about? Ride Dusty this afternoon? It was so cold outside that I would have to wear four layers of clothes, and at that rate, I knew I would be so bundled up, I wouldn't be able to get on my pony, much less stay on.

"But Daddy. . .what if it only gets up to zero again like it did yesterday?"

He shrugged. "So? It won't be that cold in the barn."

"The barn?"

"We don't milk the cows in the afternoon. You can ride her up and down the barn aisle."

I stared at my father, considering what he had said.

Ride Dusty in the barn? Up and down the center aisle?

Dad grinned. "Didn't think of that, did you." He reached for his cup of coffee. "I guess I didn't think of it before, either, did I."

"How come I can't ride her this morning?" I asked.

"I've got to clean the barn," he replied.

I tried to avoid being out in the barn when the barn cleaner was running. Normally I didn't mind the odor of cow manure. I had grown up with it, and it was just one of those everyday farm smells. But when the barn cleaner stirred up the manure and moved it out of the barn, the smell became downright overpowering. The barn cleaner was noisy, too, scraping and squawking and rumbling as it moved around the gutter channel to carry the manure up the chute where it would fall into the manure spreader parked outside the barn.

The rest of the morning crawled by. Just when I thought we were never going to get around to eating dinner, noon arrived. I was so excited about riding Dusty with her saddle that I could hardly swallow. I managed to eat a few bites, though. If I didn't, Mom wouldn't excuse me from the table.

After dinner, I put on my barn coat, a stocking cap, mittens and boots. It was a short walk to the barn, so I figured I wouldn't need a scarf around my face. And once I was out in the barn, I probably wouldn't need mittens. The cows usually kept the barn warm enough so I didn't have to wear mittens.

Although the little saddle wasn't very heavy, Dad carried it out to the barn for me. I walked along beside him, with an old tan rug tucked under my arm that Mom said I could use as a saddle blanket. The rug was made out of the same kind of material as a bedspread. Mom said it was called chenille. The rug also had a rubber back on it, but Dad said if we folded it in half, that it would work all right.

The steady crunch and squeak of our footsteps in the snow accompanied us across the yard. The day was blindingly bright and sunny, but a strong breeze blew out of the west, and the air was so cold that my cheeks stung.

When we reached the barn, the frosted hinges creaked and squealed as Dad opened the door. If the temperature dropped below zero overnight and it stayed below freezing during the day, the hinges became coated with a thick layer of frost.

Once we were inside the barn, the warmth was a welcome relief for my tingling cheeks. Dad had let the cows outside for a while this morning but had put them back in again so their udders wouldn't freeze. Some of the cows were eating hay and some were taking a nap. When the cows shifted in their stalls, the stanchions jingled, and I could hear the sound of running water as one pushed her nose into the watering cup beside her to get a drink. The water cups looked like army helmets with a paddle in the middle. When a cow pushed her nose against the paddle, water would gush into the cup.

As Dad closed the barn door, the hinges creaked and squealed again. Now that my father was finished cleaning, the barn lime he had sprinkled on the floor made the air smell like the chalk dust from the erasers at school. Every day, the teacher picked two people to go outside and clap the erasers. During the spring and fall, everyone wanted to go outside to clean the erasers, but I had noticed that during the coldest part of winter, no one wanted to do it.

After Dad had made sure the door was latched securely, he turned and set the saddle on top of the twine barrel. I laid the rug on top of it.

"Let's bring Dusty out into the aisle," he suggested.

I went into the calf pen that was Dusty's home for the winter. The first year I had Dusty, Mom said the pony didn't belong in the barn because we needed room for calves and that Dusty could go into the chicken coop situated at this end of her pasture not far from the milkhouse.

Unfortunately—or fortunately, depending upon your point of view—Dusty refused to go into the chicken coop. When the weather was cold and windy, or if it was snowing, the pony would stand with her head inside the door, but she wouldn't go into the coop.

This year Mom said she couldn't take another winter of seeing the pony standing outside with six inches of snow piled on her back and had suggested that maybe Dad ought to make room for Dusty in the barn. Since then, Dusty had been staying in the calf pen at night and during the day, too, when it was cold out like it was today.

I snapped the lead onto the pony's halter and led her into the center aisle. In just a few minutes, I would finally have a chance to use my brand new saddle. The pony had been a dream come true, and now the saddle was a second dream come true. I felt like pinching myself, just to be sure that I wasn't imagining the whole thing.

"Well, Dusty," Dad said, "let's see what you think of your new saddle."

The pony sniffed the rug Mom said I could use as a saddle blanket and allowed it to be placed on her back. Then she accepted the saddle without protest, too, although she turned her head a couple of times to see what we were doing.

"How do you know how to put a saddle on?" I asked.

Dad shrugged. "It wasn't so long ago that we used horses for everything. I could still harness a team in no time flat, too, if I had the opportunity."

I knew that when Loretta and Ingman were little, Dad had used work horses to farm and that sometimes my brother and sister had ridden the work horses. I had always thought it was terribly unfair that I had been born after Dad started using tractors to do the farm work. Riding the big work horses would have been tremendous fun.

I watched intently as Dad threaded the length of leather through the metal ring on the girth, drew it up, and then circled it around and back down through the loop. If I paid close enough attention, maybe I could learn how to do it myself pretty soon.

Dad reached down to check the girth. "You have to be sure this is back far enough so it doesn't rub when she walks. Otherwise she'll get sores from it," he explained.

When Dad was satisfied that the saddle was girthed properly, I stepped back to admire Dusty's brand new riding gear.

I blinked once. . .twice. . .then I moved around to the other side.

Somehow, the saddle did not look at all the way I had expected. From watching western shows on television, I knew what a saddle was supposed to look like when it was on a horse—and this wasn't it.

I glanced over at Dad and saw he was pursing his lips, which meant that he wanted to grin, or even to laugh out loud, but knew he shouldn't.

Under my father's care and guidance—which meant he never missed an opportunity to toss Dusty another flake of hay or an extra handful of the ground corn and oats that we fed the cows—she had become an exceptionally plump pony. She was also taller than a regular Shetland pony. Or maybe I should say she was taller than the Shetland ponies that went around and around in a circle at the fair in town every June.

Standing there with the brand-new saddle perched on her back, Dusty reminded me of those circus elephants I had seen on television that were wearing a tiny piece of square cloth for the pretty ladies in the spangled leotards to sit on.

I wasn't sure if I wanted to laugh or cry.

"Daddy!" I gasped. "How am I going to ride Dusty like that? She looks like...well...she looks like..."

"A fat pony with a fly on her back?" Dad suggested.

"Daddy! She doesn't look *that* bad!"

My father, who was still pursing his lips and trying not to laugh out loud, jiggled the saddle back and forth. "You don't have to worry about riding her. It'll stay on. . .I think."

"You *think*?"

"No, no," Dad said hastily. "It'll stay on. Climb up and we'll see if we need to adjust the stirrups."

I put my foot in the stirrup and pulled myself up into the saddle.

"See?" Dad said. "I told you it would stay on."

My father lengthened out the stirrups a little bit, and two minutes later, Dusty and I were on our way.

By the time I reached the other end of the barn, I had already decided it didn't matter what Dusty looked like. I was riding my pony with a real saddle! Just like a real cowboy!

For the next hour, I had a grand time riding up and down the barn aisle, although I have to admit it felt as if I were jouncing around on a fifty-five gallon drum.

When I was finished, Dad helped me take the saddle off.

"Did it slide back and forth too much?" he asked.

I thought about that for a moment. "A little bit. It didn't really slide, but it felt wiggly."

Dad nodded. "Saddles are supposed to fit down over a horse's withers. But Dusty's too plump. This one just sits on top."

I put Dusty back in the calf pen, where she immediately started nibbling hay.

"How did the saddle feel?" Dad asked as I shut the gate and latched it. "I mean, did it feel too big or too small when you were sitting in it?"

I considered the question. "It felt just right."

"Good," Dad said. "That's the important thing. I think a big saddle for a horse would be too big for Dusty, and I bet it would be too big for you, too."

After that, whenever I had a chance—and if Dad and Ingman weren't milking, of course, because when they were milking, there were too many obstacles in the aisle—I would get Dusty out and ride her in the barn.

The first time my big brother saw Dusty wearing her brand new saddle, he laughed out loud. Ingman worked at the creamery in town six miles away, and depending upon the shift (7 p.m. to 3 p.m.; 3 p.m. to 11 p.m.; 11 p.m. to 7 a.m.), sometimes it was several days before he and I were in the barn at the same time.

"That saddle looks so tiny!" Ingman exclaimed. "Dusty, you're getting fat! How much have you been feeding her, Dad?"

My father shrugged. "Oh, not so awful much. Whenever I feed the cows, I throw a little more hay in for her, and I give her a couple handfuls of ground feed, too, I guess."

From then on, my father figured maybe he'd better put my pony on a diet. He only fed her half as much feed and not as much hay. As far as I could tell, it didn't seem to make a difference.

When the weather grew warmer, I put the saddle on Dusty and instead of riding up and down the barn aisle, we went riding up and down the driveway. And when spring arrived, we rode around the farm and up and down the dirt road too. Then during the summer, Dusty and I traveled the three-quarters of a mile to our other place so I could help Dad with the haying.

And when our new neighbors bought a small, pure black pony who escaped from his pasture once or twice a week, I felt more like a cowboy than ever as I saddled my pony and set off down the driveway. No matter how often we had to do it, Dusty willingly trotted to the other neighbor's hayfield so we could lure Smokey Joe back home where he belonged. Smokey Joe liked Dusty so much that he would have followed her anywhere.

Eventually I got used to the way my plump brown pony looked with the little saddle perched on her broad back. But when I led Dusty to the granary steps so I could get on more easily, the grins on the faces of the milk hauler or the insurance salesman or the guy who delivered gasoline to our farm told me that she still looked much the same as she had the first time we saddled her.

Didn't matter to me.

As Mom was fond of saying, beauty is in the eye of the beholder, and in my opinion, Dusty always remained the best and smartest pony in the whole world.

Even if she did resemble a circus elephant when she wore that saddle.

****

~ 20 ~
A New Year Unlike Any Other

Only this morning the Christmas tree had stood by the living room picture window in all its glory. But now it was gone.

When Loretta carried the box of ornaments upstairs to the closet where they would stay until next year, an empty feeling settled in the pit of my stomach. Tomorrow school started again. And that meant Christmas vacation was over.

Happy New Year, indeed.

According to what I had read in Loretta's magazines (*Ladies' Home Journal* and *Redbook*, to name two), some people went to fancy New Year's Eve parties where the men dressed in black tuxedos and the women wore glittering ball gowns as pretty as the roses my sister had planted that bloomed in our front yard every summer.

In our family, however, we celebrated the holiday by eating a New Year's Day dinner that rivaled the dinner we ate at Thanksgiving and Christmas. Turkey or ham or pot roast. Mashed potatoes. Gravy. Candied carrots. Creamed corn. Pickled beets. Dill pickles. Cranberry sauce. Homemade buns. And pie for dessert: lemon meringue, apple, blueberry, blackberry, custard or banana cream. Sometimes we even had two kinds of pie.

But after we had finished eating dinner, taking down the tree was the grand finale to our New Year's Day celebration. As far as my mother was concerned, New Year's marked the end of Christmas, and we were never able to convince her otherwise. On January first, the Christmas decorations were supposed to come down. And that was that.

So today, after the dinner dishes had been washed and put away, Loretta and I had taken the tinsel, ornaments and lights off the tree and packed it all into the big box where we kept the Christmas decorations. And then Dad had carried the tree outside.

When my sister brought in the vacuum cleaner to clean up the pine needles littering the floor, an odd echo bounced around the room. Even our footsteps echoed. Without the Christmas tree in the empty space by the picture window, each small noise seemed hollow.

After Loretta finished vacuuming, we pushed Mom's chair back to its spot in front of the window. As we returned the other pieces of furniture to their rightful places, the echoes stopped all together, and in a little while, the room looked as if Christmas had never happened at all.

Before the Christmas decorations had been taken down, I hadn't thought much about school. Now that the living room looked the way it did at other times of the year, I could no longer ignore that the end of vacation had arrived.

And once school started, all I had to look forward to was at least three more months of bitter cold and snow.

Which meant endless days of trudging around in winter boots and a heavy coat.

With the added burden of keeping track of my mittens and a hat.

That's not to say we didn't have winter before Christmas vacation. Sometimes as early as the first part of November, snow began covering the landscape, adding layer upon layer of white. And some years by mid-December, we had so much snow that Dad could no longer drive into the fields with the tractor and manure spreader. December sometimes turned bitterly cold, too, when the thermometer would fall to twenty degrees below zero overnight and then it would only warm up to ten below or zero the next day.

But this New Year's Day—as it turned out—was completely different from all the others I had known. Instead of the typical winter weather, the temperature was in the upper 40s. What little snow we'd gotten earlier had all melted. There wasn't a flake in sight. A brown lawn in January, and brown fields and hills stretching in all directions, was something I had never seen before.

Still, the novelty of riding my bike on New Year's Day didn't make me feel any better about going back to school. Usually I would have spent my last afternoon of vacation sliding down the driveway on my sled; since we didn't have any snow, I decided to ride my bike. And yet, I was painfully aware that each trip around the buildings past the machine shed, the granary, the barn, the garage and then the machine shed again brought the end of vacation just that much closer.

During Christmas vacation, I felt as free as I did during the summer. The two-week break for the holidays meant I could be in the barn with Dad whenever I wanted. That I could ride to town with him in the pickup truck when he went to grind feed. That I could play with my dog, Needles, or ride my pony, Dusty, all afternoon.

Going back to school meant an abrupt end to my freedom. Instead of working on penmanship, or arithmetic problems, or the assignments in the reading workbook, I would much rather be at the farm where really exciting things happened. Newborn calves, for instance, who needed someone to dry them off and look after them while they took their first tottering steps.

I had no more than started on another trip around the buildings with my bicycle when I thought of something that cheered me up so much I forgot to pedal. It was a *wonderful* idea. Just the thing to make me feel better about going back to school tomorrow.

Now all I had to do was convince my mother.

When my bicycle had almost coasted to a stop near the barn, I hopped off and headed for the machine shed to put it away. Then I ran to the house and leaped up the porch steps. I yanked open the door but then stopped to catch my breath. I absolutely could not look as if I were in a hurry. It would be just the sort of thing to make my mother wonder what I was up to.

Several minutes later, I sauntered into the living room.

"It's really nice today, isn't it Mom?" I said, gazing out of the picture window where the Christmas tree had stood so recently. An easterly breeze rustled the bare branches of the silver maple that had been planted before my mother was born. If I squinted my eyes, I could almost convince myself that instead of hazy January sunshine, it was spring sunshine warming the bare, brown lawn.

"Why—yes, it is a nice day," my mother replied as she threaded her embroidery needle with a length of floss.

"Hardly seems like winter at all, does it?" I continued, casually clasping my hands behind my back as I turned toward my mother.

"Nooooo...it doesn't," she replied, steel-blue eyes narrowing behind her reading glasses.

I could tell that she was already getting suspicious about where the conversation was leading.

"I can't hardly believe all the snow has melted!" I exclaimed.

Mom didn't reply this time. She just looked at me steadily, lips pursed, waiting for what I would say next.

"Since it's so warm and we don't have any snow on the ground, it would be *really* pointless for me to wear boots, mittens and a hat to school tomorrow, wouldn't it?" I asked.

My mother jabbed the threaded embroidery needle into the pillowcase she was working on. She had finished all of the flowers and now she was doing the leaves.

"Forget it," she said. "It's January, and no child of mine is going to school without boots, mittens and a hat."

Somehow, I had known all along that's how she would feel about it.

"But Mom," I continued, "I bet none of the *other* kids will be wearing boots and mittens and hats."

That, of course, was the wrong thing to say.

"And I suppose you mean to tell me if all the other kids jumped off a cliff, you'd want to do it, too?" she replied.

"No, no, I wouldn't do that," I said.

I thought for a few moments, trying to find another argument which would appeal to her.

"But Mom," I said, "if I wear boots and mittens and a hat, I'll get all sweaty when I go out at recess. It's not good to be sweaty in the winter. I might catch a chill."

My mother frowned and stopped embroidering.

I waited for her to consider what might happen if I got too warm and then became chilled. Mom always warned me that I shouldn't go outside in the winter without a coat because if I got chilled, I might catch pneumonia.

"Well," she said at last, "well...I suppose when it's warm like this, and we don't have any snow, boots *might* be kind of pointless."

I felt like jumping up and down and clapping my hands, although I knew that I still had to play it cool.

"So—you mean I don't have to wear boots, mittens and a hat tomorrow?"

"No. I guess not," Mom replied as she started embroidering again. "If the weather is like it is today, you don't have to wear boots."

I noticed she didn't say anything about the mittens and the hat, but I let it go. Boots were a major victory.

During the winter, my life seemed to revolve around snow boots. Put them on in the morning before leaving for school. Take them off at school. Put them on before recess. Take them off after recess. Put them on before going home. Take them off at home. Put them on before going outside to play. Take them off when coming back into the house. I spent so much time changing back and forth between boots and shoes that I was amazed I ever got anything else done—like learning to read or memorizing my multiplication tables.

But tomorrow would be different. Tomorrow I wouldn't have to wear boots. Tomorrow my feet could be as free as they were in the spring or the summer or the fall when I wore ordinary shoes.

"Thanks, Mom," I said, giving her a big hug.

A smile flitted across my mother's lips, there and gone, like a sparrow grabbing a piece of oats from the granary floor.

"Yes, well," she replied. "Contrary to what you think, I *do* remember what it was like to wear boots to school."

For the rest of the day and all that evening, I had to keep reminding myself it wasn't something I had dreamed, that Mom had actually said I didn't have to wear boots to school tomorrow.

I fell asleep that night thinking about how wonderful it was going to be when I didn't have to wear boots.

And of course, my first thought the next morning when I opened my eyes was, 'I don't have to wear boots to school today!'

I jumped out of bed.

I glanced out the window.

In an instant, my anticipation vanished.

Gone. Poof. Kaput.

Just like that.

The world outside my bedroom window was covered in white. And it was still snowing. I could barely see across the driveway, although I knew the faint patches of yellow where the barn ought to be meant that Dad had turned the barn lights on and was doing the milking.

Since yesterday afternoon when Mom had said I didn't have to wear boots to school, I had never once considered that it might snow overnight. The gentle breeze that had rustled the maple branches the day before had turned into a howling wind that was piling snow ahead of it in rippling drifts.

I tromped downstairs into the kitchen, my shoulders feeling as if they each weighed fifty pounds.

"Mom!" I said, when I reached the bottom step. "It's SNOWING!"

"Yes, it is," my mother replied as she finished pouring her first cup of morning coffee. "Dad says we've got eight inches already, so I guess I'd better turn on the radio to see if there's school today."

A little while later I headed out the door, bundled in boots, a heavy coat, mittens and a hat.

"*Yipeeeee!!*" I shouted, as I waded through the snowdrifts on my way out to the barn to see Dad.

Funny, isn't it, how one little sentence can really make your day? "The following schools are closed…"

Of course by the next morning, the roads had been cleared and once again, I found myself on the way to school—wearing the detested boots, along with my winter coat, mittens and a hat.

All was not lost, however.

Yes, I had missed my one and only opportunity not to wear boots, but at least I'd had another day of vacation.

And one more day of Christmas vacation, I decided, was even better than not wearing boots.

****

Appendix A

Traditional Norwegian Christmas Recipes

~ How to Make Lefse ~

When I was a kid growing up on our small dairy farm in Wisconsin that had been homesteaded by Norwegian immigrants in the late 1800s, I figured everyone knew how to make lefse. After all, everyone I knew could make lefse, so didn't that mean everyone else could make it too?

That was forty years ago.

Now I know better.

In the rural area where I live, however, at least a few people still do know how to make lefse. And at Christmas, you can even buy lefse in some of the grocery stores around here.

Several years ago, a girl from Norway was a foreign exchange student at the local high school. When she found out some people in Wisconsin still make lefse and that we consider it a delicious delicacy, she expressed amazement. "I can't believe you make that yet. We've don't do it anymore in Norway," she said.

'What?' I thought. 'No lefse?! What's the matter with those Norwegians?'

During the latter part of the 1800s, 30,000 Norwegians immigrated to Wisconsin. Today, nearly a half million people are their descendants out of a total population of 5.5 million. In other words, almost 10 percent of Wisconsin residents are of Norwegian descent.

Expert lefse makers use a lefse griddle (a large, round electric griddle that heats up to 500 degrees), a grooved lefse rolling pin, and flat wooden lefse turners. But you don't have to buy special equipment to make lefse. You can use ordinary kitchen utensils: an electric fry pan (that heats up to 400 or 450 degrees Fahrenheit), a rolling pin, a pancake turner, and a large mixing bowl. You will also need potatoes, butter or margarine, a little sugar, some milk, and flour.

Rolling lefse is a skill that requires plenty of patience and lots of practice. Expert lefse makers produce pieces that are as large as the top of a snare drum and practically thin enough to read a newspaper through. My lefse, which turns out just like my mother's did, is about the size of a dinner plate and somewhat thicker.

Lefse experts recommend ricing the cooked potatoes, but my mother always mashed the potatoes. Refrigerating the mashed or riced potatoes overnight makes the lefse easier to roll out.

When you're ready to start making lefse, take the potatoes out of the refrigerator and mash or rice them again. I have one of those crisscross patterned potato mashers, and it works well for taking the lumps out of the mashed potatoes. Lefse rolls out easier if the dough is cold, so make sure the potatoes are cold when you start. You may also want to refrigerate the dough for a while after you mix it. I have noticed that when I reach the end of the batch and the dough is starting to warm up, the lefse is harder to roll out.

Making a batch of lefse from this recipe takes about one and a half hours and will yield approximately two dozen pieces, depending upon how much dough you use for each one.

Here is my mother's lefse recipe:

Lefse
• 4 heaping cups of mashed or riced potatoes
• 1 stick of butter (or margarine)
• 1/3 cup of milk
• 1 teaspoon of sugar
• 1 teaspoon of salt
• 2 cups of flour
• extra flour for rolling out the dough.

Measure out the mashed/riced potatoes into a large mixing bowl. In a medium-sized saucepan, melt the butter/margarine in the milk; stir in the sugar and salt. Then pour over the cold mashed (riced) potatoes and mix.

Stir two cups of flour into the potato mixture. The dough will be sticky and soft.

Start heating the griddle or electric frying pan. Do not add any oil, margarine or shortening. Lefse is baked on a dry surface.

Take a lump of dough about the size of an egg. Place a heaping teaspoon of flour on the surface where you're going to roll out your lefse. Work about half of the heaping teaspoon of flour into the lump of dough (enough so you can handle the dough, but not so much that the dough becomes dry).

Starting in the center, roll outward until the lefse is about the size of a dinner plate. Try not to roll the lefse so thin that you cannot pick it up. If the lefse tears when you start to pick it up, gather it into a lump and roll it out again. Don't do this too many times, though, or your lefse will end up tough and dry. Ideally, you should only roll the lefse once, although that's probably not a realistic expectation if you've never made lefse before. Also try to turn the lefse only once while you are rolling it out. If the lefse starts to stick, add a little more flour.

When you have the lefse rolled out, transfer it to the hot griddle. Carefully pick it up and quickly move it. If you move slowly, the lefse is more likely to tear. Expert lefse makers use flat lefse turners (they look like long flat sticks) to transfer the dough by rolling it onto the turner and then unrolling it onto the griddle. You can also try rolling your lefse onto the rolling pin and transferring it to the griddle or the fry pan.

Once you have the lefse on the griddle, bake it for about a minute, just until brown 'freckles' start to appear; then turn the lefse over and let the other side bake just until brown freckles start to appear. While the first piece of lefse is baking, roll out your second one.

After the first piece of lefse is done, use the pancake turner to remove it from the griddle and place it on a clean dishtowel. Cover with another dishtowel.

Bake the second lefse and roll out the third piece.

When the second lefse is finished, place it on top of the first one and cover with the towel again. Then bake the third piece.

Repeat until you have baked all of the dough. Place each newly baked lefse on top of the previously baked lefse and cover the stack with the towel.

Once the lefse is completely cool, place it in a plastic bag or wrap it with plastic wrap or aluminum foil to help keep it moist. You must wait until the lefse is completely cool before wrapping it, otherwise the heat from the lefse will condense inside of the plastic or the aluminum foil, and your lefse will end up soggy. If you leave the lefse overnight without wrapping it in plastic or aluminum foil, it will probably be dried out in the morning. If the lefse dries out, sprinkle a little water on the dishtowel and wrap the dishtowel and the lefse in plastic. The lefse will soften up again.

When you're ready to eat a piece of lefse, spread it with butter (or margarine), sprinkle sugar on it (some people also like to sprinkle cinnamon on their lefse), and roll into a log.

Also, once the lefse is cool, it can be frozen.

****

~ Julekake and Christmas Bread ~

In addition to making lefse for Christmas, my mother made julekake and Christmas bread. The difference between julekake and Christmas bread is that julekake is a richer bread.

Julekake
This recipe makes two large round loaves.
• 2 cups milk
• 1 cup sugar
• 1/2 cup butter (or margarine)
• 2 packages of yeast
• 1/2 cup warm water
• 1 teaspoon salt
• 1 teaspoon cardamom (substitute cinnamon or nutmeg if you prefer)
• 7 cups flour
• 1 cup of raisins
• 1/2 cup of citron
• 1/2 cup of red candied cherries
• 1/2 cup of green candied cherries

In a medium saucepan, heat the butter, milk, sugar and salt until the margarine/butter has melted. Pour the milk mixture into a large bowl and let it cool.

Dissolve the yeast in the warm water and add it to the milk mixture. Add the cardamom (or other spice) and 3 cups of flour and beat until smooth. Mix in the fruit and 4 cups of flour. Knead the dough for about 10 minutes. If the dough becomes too sticky, knead in another 1/4 to 1/2 cup of flour.

Put the dough in a greased bowl and cover and let it rise in a warm place until doubled, or about one hour.

Punch down the dough and divide in half. Knead for a minute or so, and then form each half into rounds. Place the dough on a large greased cookie sheet and let rise for 45 minutes. (The loaves will become very large, so be careful not to put them too close to the edge of the cookie sheet.)

Bake at 350 degrees for 40 to 45 minutes. If the loaves start turning too brown, turn the oven down to 325. After you remove the loaves from the oven, brush them with shortening while they are still hot. This will help the crust to stay soft. Remove loaves from the cookie sheet. Allow the julekake to cool before slicing.

If you prefer, after the julekake is cool, drizzle on powdered sugar icing and decorate with cherries, walnuts or pecans.

Christmas Bread
This recipe makes two loaves.
• 2 cups warm water
• 2 packages of dry yeast
• 1/4 cup sugar
• 1 teaspoon salt
• 2 eggs
• 1/2 cup shortening (I have also used Canola oil)
• 1 to 2 cups of citron (if you really like the taste of citron, add 2 cups)
• 6 to 7 cups of flour

Dissolve yeast in warm water. Add 2 cups of flour, sugar, eggs, salt, shortening/oil and beat until smooth. Add citron. Add 4 cups of flour. Mix. Knead for 10 minutes. If dough becomes too sticky, knead in another 1/2 to 1 cup of flour. Let rise in a warm place for 45 minutes to an hour. Punch down dough. Knead for a minute or two. Shape into loaves. Place in greased loaf pans and let rise for 45 minutes. Bake at 350 degrees for 40 to 45 minutes. Turn out of pans. Allow the bread to cool before slicing it.

****

~ "Sot Suppe" ~
(Sweet Soup)

When my mother was a child, sweet soup was a traditional part of Christmas Eve, served cold with julekake, lefse, Christmas bread, or open-faced sandwiches. Sweet Soup is made with dried fruit and tapioca. Here is how my mother told me to make sot suppe.

Sot Suppe
• 6 cups water
• 1/3 cup sugar
• 1 tablespoon quick-cooking tapioca
• 1/4 to 1/2 teaspoon cinnamon (depending upon how well you like the taste of cinnamon; you can also use a cinnamon stick)
• 2 cups dried fruit (use any kind you like: apples, apricots, peaches or a mixture of dried fruit)
• 1 cup raisins (dark or golden)
• 1 cup dried prunes
• 1 tablespoon lemon juice (you can also use 1 teaspoon of dried lemon rind or several slices of fresh lemon)

In a medium saucepan, combine the sugar, tapioca, cinnamon and water. Bring to boiling, stirring constantly. Stir in fruit (including the lemon if you're using sliced lemon) and heat to boiling again. Cover. Simmer for 15 minutes, or until the fruit is tender.

After the fruit is tender, if you're using lemon juice, stir in the lemon juice (or teaspoon of dried lemon rind). Serve either cold or warm, depending upon your preference. If you use a sliced lemon, remove the lemon rind before serving.

For a light afternoon 'Norwegian' lunch (after hiking, sledding, snowshoeing or cross-country skiing), serve sweet soup with Julekake or Christmas bread, Christmas cookies, open-faced sandwiches, and a variety of sliced cheeses.

****

~ Lutefisk ~

Lutefisk (loo-ta-fisk) means "lye fish"—or in other words, cod soaked in potash lye. (Sounds yummy, doesn't it?) As long as I am including a few recipes for traditional Norwegian Christmas foods, I would be remiss if I didn't mention lutefisk. But that's all I'm going to do is mention it. My mother would not even allow lutefisk in the house, never mind fixing it or eating it. "I ate enough of it when I was a kid. That was a good, big plenty," she'd say.

When my mother was a child, blocks of frozen lutefisk would be stored in the shed. This was before there was electricity on our farm, so of course, there was no freezer.

"My mother would go out with the ax and would chop off a hunk. And that's what we'd eat for supper. Even the thought of smelling boiling lutefisk makes my stomach turn," my mother would recall.

Every time Mom talked about lutefisk, she would look as though she had just smelled something offensive. A skunk maybe. Or a baby's dirty diaper. Or the scrap pail when it needed to be soaked in bleach again. She also got the same look on her face, incidentally, when talking about blood sausage.

After I was an adult, I decided I ought to try eating some lutefisk so I could make up my own mind about it. Lutefisk tastes like fish (sort of). It's the texture that bothers me. (Imagine eating slimy rubber.) If you soak it in enough melted butter, that helps disguise some of the texture.

When I told Mom I thought lutefisk tasted pretty much like fish, she informed me that what's available in the store now isn't 'real' lutefisk. "I don't think they actually soak it in lye anymore. If they did, no one would eat it," she said.

As far as I'm concerned, soaking fish in a substance derived from wood ashes and which was used to make soap doesn't sound like an especially good idea. But that's just my opinion. There are plenty of people around my hometown who would choose lutefisk over lobster or tenderloin or a Porterhouse steak.

****

~ Fattigman ~

Fattigman (pronounced "futty-mun") is a deep-fried Norwegian cookie that my sister made sometimes when I was a kid and that was also served after the Sunday school Christmas program. Fattigman means "poor man's cookies" or "poor man's donuts."

Fattigman
• 6 egg yolks
• 1/3 cup sugar
• 1/2 cup cream
• 1 tablespoon brandy (or 1 teaspoon brandy extract)
• 1 teaspoon cardamom (or nutmeg; my mother often substituted nutmeg in recipes that called for cardamom)
• 1/4 teaspoon salt
• 2 to 3 cups flour

Beat egg yolks and sugar on high speed with an electric mixer for five minutes. Stir in cream, brandy, and cardamom. Mix in enough flour to make a stiff dough. Roll dough very thin and cut into two-inch by two-inch pieces. Cut a slit in the middle and pull one of the points through the slit. Deep-fry until golden brown. When cool, sprinkle with powdered sugar. I put powdered sugar in a plastic container with a cover, add some fattigman and shake gently to coat them.

****

Appendix B

Christmas Cookies

~ Loretta's Mothball Cookies ~
(as mentioned in the story "Good Things Come in Small Packages")

- 1 cup of butter
- 1/4 cup of powdered sugar
- 1 teaspoon vanilla
- 2 cups flour
- 1/4 teaspoon salt
- 2 cups chopped nuts

Combine ingredients. Chill one hour. Form into small balls. Place on greased cookie sheet. Bake at 250 degrees for one hour. Roll in powdered sugar while still warm and again when cool.

****

~ **Loretta's Chocolate Bonbons** ~
(as mentioned in the story "Good Things Come in Small Packages")

- 1 1/2 cups shredded coconut
- 1 stick butter
- 2 pounds powdered sugar
- 1 can sweetened condensed milk
- 2 cups chopped nuts
- 1 1/2 teaspoons vanilla
- 1 large package chocolate chips
- 2/3 bar paraffin

(Instead of chocolate chips and paraffin, the coconut balls can be dipped in melted chocolate almond bark.)

Mix coconut, butter, powdered sugar, condensed milk, nuts and vanilla. Roll into small balls. Chill in refrigerator for several hours or in the freezer for one hour. Melt chocolate chips and paraffin in a double boiler (or in a clean coffee can set on canning jar rings in a pan of water). Using a toothpick, dip the chilled coconut balls into the chocolate mixture. Place on wax paper until set.

****

~ Filled Cookies ~

Cookies with a date filling were my dad's favorite kind.

• 3/4 cup butter or margarine (softened)
• 3/4 cup shortening
• 2 cups sugar
• 3 eggs
• 2 teaspoons vanilla
• 5 cups flour
• 1 teaspoon baking powder
• 1/2 teaspoon salt
• several tablespoons of milk if the dough seems too dry
• Jam: blackberry, black raspberry, strawberry, red raspberry, plum conserve, apple conserve, or date filling (the recipes for plum and apple conserve and date filling are included on the next page)

Heat oven to 350 degrees. Cream butter, margarine, sugar, eggs and vanilla. Stir in flour, baking powder and salt. If the dough is too dry, add 1 or 2 tablespoons of milk. If the dough seems too wet, add 1/4 or 1/2 cup of flour.

Roll out dough. Use either a small round cookie cutter or one large round cutter. Place cookies on an ungreased baking sheet. Put one teaspoon of jam (or other filling) in the middle of the smaller rounds or off to one side of the larger rounds. Place another small round on top of the small rounds; fold the larger rounds in half. Use a fork to crimp the edges together and to poke holes in the top. Bake for 15 minutes, or until light brown.

This recipe makes about six dozen filled cookies.

The recipe can also be used to make cut-out Christmas cookies frosted with colored icing.

****

~ Plum Conserve ~

If plum conserve is made specifically for filling cookies, store any that remains in the refrigerator and use on toast or biscuits. The conserve can also be sealed in pint jars. (This recipe makes about three pints.)

• 8 to 10 fresh, large, ripe plums
• 1/2 cup of water
• 4 cups of sugar
• 2 cups of raisins
• 1 cup chopped walnuts
• 2 tablespoons of lemon juice

Pit the plums and chop into small pieces. Place in a large saucepan and add the sugar and water. Boil for 10 minutes, stirring constantly. Add the lemon juice, raisins and walnuts and cook for 10 minutes longer, stirring constantly. **(Note: Recipe can also be made using 3 cups of chopped apples instead of plums. Add 1/2 teaspoon of cinnamon.)**

~ Date Filling ~

• 3 cups chopped dates
• 1/2 cup sugar
• 1 2/3 cups water
• 1 tablespoon lemon juice

Put all ingredients into a saucepan and cook over low heat, stirring constantly, until thickened (10 or 15 minutes).

****

~ Old-Fashioned Sugar Cookies ~

This recipe can be used to make cut-out cookies or you can roll tea-spoons of dough into balls, dip in sugar, and then flatten with the bottom of a water glass dipped in sugar.

Old-Fashioned Sugar Cookies
• 1/2 cup of butter, margarine, or other shortening
• 1 cup sugar
• 2 eggs
• 1 tablespoon of cream (or Half & Half)
• 2 1/4 cups of flour
• 1 1/2 teaspoons of baking powder
• 1/2 teaspoon of nutmeg
• 1 1/2 teaspoons of lemon extract (I have also used lemon juice; if you want a less lemony taste to the cookies, use lemon juice)

Cream together shortening (butter or margarine), sugar, eggs and cream. Mix in the dry ingredients and the lemon extract or the lemon juice. Work the dough with your hands for a minute before rolling out the cookies.

Bake on an ungreased baking sheet at 350 degrees for 10 minutes.

A single recipe makes about three dozen cookies.

****

Appendix C

How To Make Candles Using Old Crayons
(as featured in the story "A Candle For Christmas")

Materials:
- 1 wax carton (quart) (milk, fabric softener, or orange juice)
- 1 pound of paraffin wax
- 4 or 5 old crayons
- two trays of ice cubes
- a double boiler (or an empty coffee can and a saucepan)
- 1 piece of ordinary white package string about six inches long.

Caution: *Do not heat paraffin directly over the burner. Paraffin is easily combustible. Use a double boiler or a two-pound coffee can set in a pan of water. I put the coffee can on top of home canning jar rings (the rings, not the flat lids). If the can is not set on top of something, the concave bottom creates a vacuum when the water begins to heat up, plus if it's on the bottom of the pan, it's just that much closer to the burner.*

Trim the top part of the carton off so that what remains is about six inches high.

Cut the string so that it is six inches long. (To make a wick that lasts longer, try braiding three pieces of string together.)

Melt the paraffin wax over medium heat in a double boiler or a coffee can in a pan of water. Use three-quarters of a pound for a somewhat smaller candle or use all four squares for a larger candle. Once the water begins to boil, it will take 10 or 15 minutes for the paraffin to melt.

Break the crayons into small pieces and add to the paraffin. If the crayons are added first before the wax is melted, the color makes it difficult to see if all of the paraffin is liquefied.

Use a pair of tongs (a scissors works, too), and dip the string into the paraffin. Dipping the string will ensure that it is coated with paraffin since the ice cubes may prevent some sections from coming in contact with the liquid wax. Hold the string so that it is in the middle of the carton and fill the carton with ice cubes. Pour the hot paraffin over the ice cubes.

The candle will be set in about 30 minutes. Let the candle stand for another hour or two until most of the ice cubes are melted. Pour off the water. Peel off the carton. Place the candle in a tray or on a plate to catch the rest of the water from the ice cubes as they finish melting. Let the candle dry for a day or two.

The candles I have made with a single piece of string only burn for an hour or so and burn quickly enough so that most of the paraffin remains intact. To use the paraffin again, melt the candle and pour the wax into other containers to make solid candles.

~ Solid Candles ~

To make solid candles, select several glass containers. Pint or half-pint canning or jelly jars work well. For the wick, measure out a few more inches of string than is needed to reach the bottom of the container. Tie the string around a pencil. Put the pencil across the top of the container to hold the wick in place. When the paraffin and crayons are melted, pour the liquid wax into the container(s). When the candle is set, snip off the wick about a half inch above the wax.

~ Scented Candles ~

To make scented candles, put three or four teaspoons of vanilla extract into the bottom of the double boiler (or the coffee can) and then add the paraffin and crayons. When the wax is melted, pour into containers.

****

~ Acknowledgements ~

First of all, I would like to express my gratitude to my brother, Ingman, and to my sister, Loretta, for allowing me to write about them. As far as I'm concerned, Ingman and Loretta are the best brother and sister any little sister could ever ask for.

Next in line is my husband, Randy. He has always been supportive of my endeavors and has encouraged me every day by telling me to "go write a book." So I did. He is the technical genius responsible for my website, www.ruralroute2.com.

Many other people also deserve a thank you. My niece, Karn Mohn. And my sister-in-law, Mary Ellen Ralph. My mother-in-law and father-in-law, Ruth and Dick Simpson. Sisters-in-law and brothers-in-law, Jeanie and Scott Simpson and Anne and Bernie Koenigs. My friends Vicki (Riemer) Freeberg; Sheila (Mittelstadt) Berger; Edith (Bauer) McKee; Anita (Hein) Stocker; and Deb Garrett. I must also include Ellis Bloomfield, the former owner of the *Colfax Messenger*, and Carlton and Paula DeWitt, the current owners of the *Messenger* and the *Glenwood City Tribune Press Reporter*, as well as Ilo Ayres, the typesetter at the *Messenger*, and Marlin Raveling, news editor at the *Messenger*. You have all helped me in your own way, and for that I say, "thank you!"

And last, but not least, I want to thank my readers—both on the Internet and in print.

Without readers, writers wouldn't have a job.

****

~ About the Author ~

LeAnn R. Ralph earned a bachelor's degree in English with a writing emphasis from the University of Wisconsin-Whitewater and a Master of Arts in Teaching from UW-Whitewater. She spent several years teaching English at a boys' boarding school and also has worked as a freelance writer and as a newspaper reporter. She is the editor of the Wisconsin Regional Writers' Assoc. quarterly publication, *The Wisconsin Regional Writer*, and lives in west central Wisconsin with her husband, Randy Simpson, in the house that her parents built when they retired from farming.

LeAnn's next book, *Give Me a Home Where the Dairy Cows Roam*, will feature another collection of stories about growing up on a dairy farm in Wisconsin. If you would like to be on a mailing list to receive notification when her next book is available—or if you would like to purchase autographed copies of *Christmas In Dairyland*—e-mail her at—bigpines@ruralroute2.com—or write to her at—E6689 970th Ave., Colfax, WI 54730-4711.

****